In or Out of The Mainstream?
Lessons from Research on Disability and Development Cooperation

Edited by
Bill Albert

THE DISABILITY PRESS
LEEDS

First published 2006 The Disability Press
Centre for Disability Studies
School of Sociology and Social Policy
University of Leeds
Leeds LS2 9JT .

Output from disk supplied and printed by University Print Services, a division of Media Services at Leeds.

British Library Cataloguing in publication Data
A catalogue record for this book is available from the British Library

Library of Congress Cataloguing in publication Data
A catalogue record of this book has been requested

ISBN 0-9549026-2-9

Contents

The Disability Press

The Disability Press aims to provide an alternative outlet for work in the field of disability studies. The Disability Press draws inspiration from the work of all those countless disabled individuals and their allies who have, over the years, struggled to put this particular issue onto the political agenda. Its establishment is a testament to the growing recognition of 'disability' as an equal opportunities and human rights issue within the social sciences.

Funding for this volume was provided by the UK's Department for International Development. The editor wishes to record his thanks to the School of Sociology and Social Policy at the University of Leeds for its continuing support of the Disability Press.

Contributors

Bill Albert was research director of the Disability KaR. He is a co-director of IDEA (The International Disability Equality Agency).

Victor Cordeiro is the Programme Manager for Action Aid India.

Shivaram Deshpande is the Programme Manager for Leonard Cheshire International, based in India.

Andrew K. Dube is CEO of Samaita-Maita Development Services (SMDS) in South Africa. He has twenty years' experiences in designing, managing, evaluating and monitoring disability programmes in Southern Africa.

Tomson Dube is the Director of Organization of Rural Associations for Progress in Zimbabwe, as well as Academic Director for the diploma programme in Disability Studies for the Pan African Institute for Development Studies.

Arne H. Eide is a Research Director at the Foundation for Scientific and Industrial Research at the Norwegian Institute of Technology (SINTEF) in Norway. He is also Professor in Rehabilitation at Sør-Trøndelag University College.

Steve Harknett has nine years' experience working in disability-related projects. His recent work has been to facilitate the formation of the Disability Development Services Pursat (DDSP), an innovative community-based organisation working with disabled people in rural Cambodia.

Mark Harrison is Director of the Social Action Research Centre, at the University of East Anglia, UK . He was the programme director of the Disability Knowledge and Research (KaR) Programme and is a co-director of IDEA.

Rabiul Hasan is Deputy Director of the Centre for Services and Information on Disability (CSID) in Bangladesh

Rachel Hurst is the Director of Disability Awareness in Action the international research and information network on disability and human rights.

Maria Kett is a Research Fellow at the Leonard Cheshire Centre of Conflict Recovery, University College London.

Richard Light has worked as head of research at Disability Awareness in Action (DAA) since 1997. He is presently the NGO representative on the UK Delegation to the Ad Hoc Committee elaborating the UN convention on the rights of disabled people.

Mitch E. Loeb, who is an epidemiologist, works as a Senior Researcher at SINTEF in Oslo, Norway.

Joshua Malinga was a founder member of Disabled Peoples' International and chairperson from 1990-94 and 1998-2002. He is presently studying for a master's degree in disability studies at the University of Cape Town.

Carol Miller is a consultant on women's human rights and gender equality. She has worked with a range of multilateral and bilateral development organisations and NGOs.

Jabulani Ncube is a consultant in disability and development. He works with Phanda Consulting in Namibia.

Trine Cecilie Riis-Hansen works with the Atlas Alliance, mainly lobbying on disability and development issues. She is the vice chair for the board of directors of the Norwegian Umbrella organisation "Forum for Environment and Development".

Sue Stubbs is a freelance disability and development consultant, currently working as Coordinator of the International Disability and Development Consortium, UK.

Rebecca Yeo works as a freelance consultant on disability and international development issues. She is currently working with International Service on a disability project in Bolivia.

Acknowledgements

The UK Government's Department for International Development (DFID) funded the research for this book as well as its publication costs. It was done as a component of the dissemination phase of its Disability Knowledge and Research Programme, part of the United Kingdom's overseas development programme. However, the findings, views and recommendations are those of the authors and do not necessarily represent those of DFID. DFID is not responsible for the contents of this research. Any comments on the research should be addressed directly to the authors or the programme director.

Full details on all aspects of the Disability Knowledge and Research Programme, as well as all the research reports, can be found at:
http://www.disabilitykar.net/index.html

For comments and further information contact:

Mark Harrison
International Disability Equality Agency (IDEA)
Social Action Research Centre
Overseas Development Group
University of East ANGLIA
Norwich, NR4 7TJ
UK
(mark.harrison@uea.ac.uk)

Acronyms

ADA – Americans with Disabilities Act
ADD – Action on Disability and Development
CABDIC –Capacity Building of People with Disability in the Community
CASE – Community Agency for Social Enquiry (South Africa)
CBMI – Christian Blind Mission International
CBR – community–based rehabilitation
CDH – Care Dependency Grant (South Africa)
CEE – Commission for Employment Equity (South Africa)
CHA – Consortium of Humanitarian Agencies (Sri Lanka)
CSOs – Civil Society Organisations
DAA – Disability Awareness in Action
DKaR – Disability Knowledge and Research Programme
DPI – Disabled Persons International
DSS - Government Department of Social Services (Bangladesh)
DDSP– Disability Development Services Pursat (Cambodia)
DFID – Department for International Development (UK)
DISTAT– Disability Statistics Database for Microcomputers
DPO – disabled people's organisation
ECOSOC – United Nations Economic and Social Council
FAMOD – Mozambican Forum of Associations of Disabled People
FEDOMA – The Federation of Disability Organizations in Malawi
FFO – Federation of Organisations of Disabled People (Norway)
FIDIDA – International Development Association of Disabled Persons
(Finland)
FRC– Family Rehabilitation Centre (Sri Lanka)
HAI –HelpAge International
HI – Handicap International
ICF – International Classification of Functioning, Disability and Health
ICIDH – International Classification of Impairments, Disabilities
and Handicaps
IDC – International Disability Caucus
IDDC – International Disability and Development Consortium
IDRM – International Disability Rights Monitor
IE – inclusive education

IFIs– international financial institutions

INDS – Integrated National Disability Strategy (South Africa)

INGO – International Non-Governmental Organisation

ITDG – Intermediate Technology Development Group

KEPA – Service Centre for Development Cooperation (Finland)

LMDS – Landmine Disability Support

MDGs – Millennium Development Goals

MFA – Ministry of Foreign Affairs (Norway)

MONLAR – The Movement for National Land and Agricultural Reform (Sri Lanka)

NCD – National Council on Disability (USA)

NGO – non–governmental organisation

PAG – Project Advisory Group (DKaR)

PLA – Participatory Learning Approach

PMG – Programme Advisory Group

PRA – Participatory Rural Appraisal

PRSP – Poverty Reduction Strategy Paper

PSA – Public Service Agreement (DFID)

PWD – People with disabilities

SAFOD – Southern African Federation of the Disabled

SAPs – Structural Adjustment Programmes

SHIA – Swedish Organisations' of Disabled Persons International Aid Association

SLF– Sewa Lanka Foundation

SWAps – sector wide approaches

TAFREN – Sri Lankan government taskforce on reconstruction

TQ – Ten Question Screening Questionnaire

UNDP – United Nations Development Programme

UNICEF – United Nations Children's Fund

UNSD – United Nations Statistics Division

WB – World Bank

WEDEC– Water Engineering and Development Centre

WG – Washington City Group

WHO – World Health Organisation

CHAPTER 1

Lessons from the Disability Knowledge and Research Programme

Bill Albert and Mark Harrison

From it's official formation in the early 1980's, getting disability meaningfully on the development agenda has been the major priority for the international disability movement (DPI–1981). It is not difficult to see why. Not only are disabled people vastly over-represented among the world's poorest people, in many instances they are not considered to be 'real' people at all. As Rachel Hurst (1999, p.24) has observed, 'There is no country in the world where disabled people's rights are not violated.' Their needs and their voices ignored, segregated in institutions, denied education, employment and family life, viewed as pariahs or mendicants, in some cases murdered with impunity ('mercy killing'), disabled people are routinely excluded and marginalized, sometimes even by other excluded and marginalized groups in both the North as well as the South. This treatment, until quite recently, was mirrored in development policy and development studies.

However, In response to continued and effective lobbying by the disability movement, from the 1990s it seemed that things had begun to change. What began as a trickle of positive statements and disability-targeted interventions over the last few years has been transformed into an apparent flood of interest in disability and development cooperation from international and national aid agencies, as well as INGOs. The World Bank, USAID, DFID, agencies from the Nordic countries, OXFAM and Save the Children are only a few of the organisations that have produced statements, policies and/or guidelines aimed at including or mainstreaming disability into their development work (Albert 2004). However, as the collection of essays in this book reveal, relatively very little of practical value has yet been achieved either to bring disabled people into the mainstream of the development process or to improve their lives. Furthermore, although many aid organisations have adopted the human-rights language and slogans of the disability movement, with few exceptions, their attitudes and actions remain rooted in a medical understanding of disability and its concomitant top-down, charity-like, 'professionals-know-best' approach to disabled people themselves.

Nonetheless, it can be argued that constructing policies are an essential first step and that changing language provides a stepping stone for transforming attitudes and culture. What is required is only time and patience. Those with a more jaundiced outlook will see the plethora of promises as little more than rhetoric employed to mask the reality of continued inaction and the borrowing of our language and slogans as a clever marketing move, especially by the large INGOs which make up the global disability industry. The contributions offered here provide critical, evidence-based analyses of many of these questions, examine what has or hasn't been achieved and make positive recommendations for assessing and taking forward the genuine needs of disabled people in the developing world.

Background and activities of the Disability KaR

The aforementioned perception of how disability was being addressed informed the creation of the DFID-funded (but independently managed) Disability Knowledge and Research Programme (Disability KaR), from which the papers in this book are drawn.

In September 2000 DFID launched its Knowledge and Research Programme on Disability and Health Care Technology (Disability KaR 2000/02). The title indicates the programme's main concern. In its last year an evaluation report was commissioned (Albert, McBride, Seddon, et. al. 2002). It found that with respect to development the focus of the programme had been far too narrow and its entire conceptual approach questionable. On the latter point, it argued that disability and technology are best understood in terms of dynamic social processes rather than the more traditional or static formulations usually employed (disability=impairment, technology=equipment or infrastructure). It made a strong argument that any successor programme should adopt a social-model understanding of and a human rights approach to disability (see Chapter 3) and that, 'Greater priority should be given to encouraging and funding those projects which clearly have the active involvement of disabled people and their organisations, and can demonstrate, through their presentation of research methodology and project monitoring and evaluation, their capacity to deliver high quality and sustainable action-research.'

The critique outlined above formed the basis for DFID sponsoring the Disability KaR Programme Phase II. It became without doubt the most ambitious, wide-ranging and innovative project on disability and development ever undertaken. The programme was managed by Overseas Development Group at the University of East Anglia (UEA) and Healthlink Worldwide. Six healthcare technology projects continued to be supported, mainly because they had been commissioned under the previous programme. In fact, over £500,000 of the £1.4 million budget (Sept.2003 – Sept.2005) was given to these projects. But the primary emphasis now shifted, in line with recommendations of the 2002 evaluation, to a broader, integrated approach to disability, poverty and development. Eventually this coalesced around questions, particularly for DFID's practice, of mainstreaming disability. With this change came, at least towards the end of the programme (see Chapter 2), the more direct involvement of disabled people and their organisations (DPOs) in both the UK and in the South.

The pivotal aspect of the new Disability KaR was the policy officer post held by Philippa Thomas. She provided expert technical analysis and day-to-day support to DFID on disability issues, while ensuring that the other parts of the programme were responsive to Department's longer-term strategic needs. Her first task was to map DFID's disability work (Thomas 2004). She concluded that although there were some excellent disability initiatives, on the whole they were scattered and mainstreaming was not yet on the agenda. This finding was echoed in another report commissioned by the programme at around the same time (Ortiz 2004). It was from this point that the mainstreaming of disability became a central concern for the entire programme.

Another of the programme's important projects was a series of roundtable forums held in Malawi, Cambodia and India. These were organised by Healthlink Worldwide and a national DPO or disability organization in each country. They were preceded and followed by an electronic discussion forum which have gave participants the opportunity to develop ideas before the meetings and keep the discussions alive after the events. A number of these continue to operate.

The overall aim was to share learning and research about disability, poverty and mainstreaming. The meetings provided an opportunity for decision makers to learn from disabled people, DPOs and organisations and institutions working on disability issues in the South. Participants also came up with practical ideas for taking forward a disability agenda. For example, the Malawi roundtable (Disability KaR 2004) developed guidelines for research as well as a list of priority topics on disability and development. These then fed directly into the Disability KaR commissioned research projects considered below. In India, the roundtable (Disability KaR 2005a) set in motion an international campaign to get disability included when the Millennium Development Goals was reviewed in September 2005. Finally, the roundtable in Cambodia (Disability KaR 2005b) came up with a series of recommendations and action plans for taking forward initiatives on inclusive education.

Other activities included a communication strategy designed by Healthlink Worldwide to disseminate the programme's outputs in a variety of forms and forums. There was a two-week training course on disability mainstreaming held at UEA which brought together leaders from the disability movements in Kenya, Fiji, Namibia, Bangladesh, Cameroon, Cambodia, the Netherlands and Malawi, as well as those working for INGOs in Kenya, Uganda and Bolivia. Finally, a separate post-programme dissemination project was funded by DFID. This involved, among other things, presentations at DFID offices in London, East Kilbride, Cambodia and India, in New York at the United Nations, at USAID, the World Bank and the Inter-American Development Bank all in Washington D.C. and well-attended international workshops in Malawi, South Africa and Oslo. A presentation of the work of the Disability KaR was also given at the World Social Forum Conference held in Venezuela. Healthlink promoted the Programme's work at a WHO meeting in Geneva and an IDDC conference in Naples.

This collection too is part of the dissemination phase of the Disability KaR. All the contributions have been drawn from a selection of the reports that formed the research heart of the programme. There were three strands to the research. The first, Enabling Disabled People In Poverty Reduction, was recommended in the 2002 Evaluation and was included in the Disability KaR's original terms of reference. It was carried out primarily by disabled researchers and overseen by the Project Advisory Group (PAG), on which there was a majority of disabled people from the North and South. The Project Officer also initiated research projects. Some of these she did herself, including her mapping and final reports, and surveys on mainstreaming disability in development in India, Cambodia and Rwanda (Disability KaR 2005c). Other research (on Uganda, South Africa, Mozambique and Cambodia) she commissioned after discussions with representatives of the disability movement in the UK and the PAG. The third group of projects were decided upon after discussions with representatives of the disability movement in Europe, Africa and Asia, as well as consultation with DPOs at the Malawi Roundtable. It was also in Malawi that disabled people and their allies set out research guidelines that formed the terms of reference for the work which was commissioned (see Chapter 2). It must be stressed that all the project reports were carried out over a very short period of time – usually four to six months – and a great deal more research remains to be done in order to explore in greater depth the many important questions raised.

The research

The collection begins with a piece by Mark Harrison and Bill Albert. Drawing on the Disability KaR report that surveyed gaps in research on disability and development (Albert, Dube, et. al. 2005), Albert argues that to undertake research which makes a lasting difference to the lives of disabled people demands an emancipatory, action-research approach. Furthermore that this needs to be led by disabled people, if appropriate working in genuine partnership with academics or other professionals. Having disabled people engaged upstream in the research process is also consistent with demands from DPOs in the North and South, as well as DFID's commitment to making research more relevant to poverty reduction by putting marginalized groups in the forefront and engaging them in all aspects of research. How this approach was applied in the Disability KaR is detailed by Harrison, who was the director of the programme in its last eighteen months. He also offers a candid overview of the problems within the programme before he took over and how these began to be resolved once disabled people assumed a leading role.

Besides embracing an emancipatory research framework, all the Disability KaR projects employed a social-model understanding of disability. The third chapter, by Rachel Hurst and Bill Albert, outlines the differences between this and the traditional medical model of disability and why the whole question is of such importance for policies and practices concerned with disability and poverty in the developing world. They maintain that the social model is such a powerful tool because it helps illuminate the fact that the roots of disabled people's exclusion and poverty do not reside in biology, but in society. The former for most people is immutable; the latter through collective action can be transformed. In the second part of the chapter they consider what makes disability a fundamental human rights issue and in turn a development issue. They show that a human rights approach offers a platform for social transformation as well as a way for disabled people to transform the sense of who they are – from stigmatised objects of charity to valued subjects of their own lives. For all people who are poor and oppressed this is a key starting point of any meaningful process of social and economic development.

The fourth and fifth chapters are given over to the mainstreaming of disability in development, the central focus of the Disability KaR in all the various parts of the programme. The first, a collaborative essay by Carol Miller and Bill Albert, compares the experience of gender and disability mainstreaming. When examining the latter, gender is a logical place to begin as among' other common features, a human rights perspective and fundamental concerns about discrimination and inequality, inform both projects. Also gender has been officially on the international development agenda for more than 10 years and is a cross-cutting issue for most aid agencies. After giving concise definitions of mainstreaming and disability equality – the ultimate goal of the process – the authors delineate eight key, practical lessons that those lobbying for the inclusion of disability can learn from what has and hasn't happened in the attempts to mainstream gender in development work.

The second mainstreaming–focused chapter is drawn from a multi-authored report by disabled researchers based in Southern Africa, the UK and Norway. After determining that disability had not been mainstreamed, even in agencies that either had the appropriate policies or that were on record as strong champions, it examines why this was the case for USAID, NORAD, DFID and the World Bank. Where possible, this was done from both a Northern and Southern perspective. The intention was to undertake a policy evaporation analysis in order to see where in the long chain from formulation of policy to implementation things had gone wrong and then to be able to suggest targeted remedial action. It didn't take long to discover that there was not a very long chain to investigate. In most cases policy had evaporated before the ink was dry. A lack of broad-based institutional commitment, a failure to grasp the concept of mainstreaming, limited funding and little practical guidance on implementation were only some of the problems uncovered. Underlying all of these is the continued and wide-spread perception that disability is essentially a medical issue. They conclude that, 'Until agency staff are given the tools to be able to view disability through a social-model lens, appeals to see it as a human rights issue that demands mainstreaming into development cooperation are likely to make little progress.'

In her chapter, on disability and poverty, Rebecca Yeo points out that the oft-heard statement about poverty and disability being locked in a vicious cycle obscures the factors common to the way in which poor people and disabled people are socially excluded. She also challenges a key assumption of the Disability KaR, that mainstreaming or inclusion in agency programmes, such as the World Bank/IMF sponsored Poverty Reduction Strategy Programmes (PRSPs) offer a way forward. This is, she argues, because it is these very programmes and the globalisation project which they underpin that has helped create and maintain poverty. Disabled people and their organisations, encouraged by INGOs, have been unquestioning and have too often legitimised the neo-liberal agenda rather than joining with other marginalised groups to oppose it. In a revealing exception to this rule, one of her informants, a leader of a disability organisation in South America, observed, 'The INGOs really do nothing to help us. They only want to bring the most vulnerable people into the process of globalisation.'

The lack of reliable statistics has been a major stumbling block to getting governments in the South and aid agencies to understand the real significance of disability as a development issue or its link with poverty. What makes this even more difficult has been the failure to agree on what is being measured – the prevalence of particular impairments or the imposition of activity limitation and social exclusion. Finally, in order to be meaningful with respect to policy, there is a need, as had been identified with respect to gender mainstreaming, for disability-disaggregated data in order to highlight the differences in the life experience of disabled people and their non-disabled peers. Arne Eide and Mitch Loeb attempt to untangle these and related questions in Chapter 7. The present work builds on their previous in-depth studies on the living conditions of disabled people in three Southern African countries (Eide and Loeb 2003a, 2003b, 2005). The research done for the Disability KaR centred on working in a participatory manner with African DPOs on a wide range of issues to do with the design, collection and ultimate use of disability statistics. An important goal was to ensure the outputs of any research served the needs identified by disabled people. This piece of research and those which preceded it are an excellent example of demand-led, collaborative research between disabled people and non-disabled professionals.

Disability mainstreaming tends to focus on the activities of aid agencies and international financial institutions. However, it is also important to consider the political and legislative environment facing disabled people within developing countries. Unless this is favourable, there will be little demand for disability-inclusive external support and a reduced ability to implement such support if it is forthcoming. This point is made by the four authors of Chapter 8 who maintain that, 'Unless disabled people are in a position to lobby their governments effectively and by doing so ensure that those governments in turn indicate to donors that disability is a key concern that needs to be mainstreamed in all the various aid instruments, disability will continue to be ignored in development cooperation.' They conclude that, with some notable exceptions, disabled people's organisations have been marginalised by lack of financial support and capacity. This has resulted in them being unable to formulate, monitor and evaluate disability legislation and policy, both at national and international levels.

South Africa is one of the two countries that the authors of Chapter 8 identify in which this kind of marginalisation has not occurred, the other being Uganda. In both the disability movement is well established and strong and disabled people are fully integrated into the political process at all levels of government. But, as shown in Andrew K. Dube's papers on disability legislation in South Africa (Chapter 9) and the PRSP process in Uganda (Chapter 10), this has not been enough to ensure that disabled people's voices have been listened to or their rights protected. In South Africa, Dube examines some of the key pieces of disability legislation and finds that while the intentions have been excellent, delivery has been exceedingly poor. As a consequence these policies have had little impact on the lives of disabled people. Because of various capacity constraints at the programme level, poor championing and inadequate monitoring, as well as a lack of finance, most of the country's progressive disability policies have evaporated early in their existence. He traces successful implementation to the few instances where there has been support from ministers or senior civil servants and/or persistent lobbying from the disability movement.

In his work on disability and the Ugandan Poverty Eradication Action Plan (PEAP), Dube points out that despite the apparent strength of the disability movement in the country, they had not been consulted in the formulation of the first two PRSP exercises. Only after intense lobbying by NUDIPU were they included in the third. The representatives found the process quite daunting. Funding and government support was inadequate and they were not given sufficient time to engage with their members on what were extremely complex issues. While some felt that their involvement was used primarily to lend legitimacy to the plan, in the end disability was included for the first time in the final document. However, it was a long way from what NUDIPU had asked for, especially with respect to mainstreaming disability. There were no specific promises on disability and by failing to include disability indicators and performance benchmarks, there was no way in which the government could be held to account. Notwithstanding his critical assessment, Dube ends his account with a series of constructive recommendations about how disability can be more effectively included in any subsequent consultative process.

Although an increasing amount of aid is being delivered directly to governments either in bi-lateral or multi-lateral packages described above, traditional programme work remains important, as does the role of INGOs in brokering it. This was the topic of Jabulani Ncube's research in Mozambique. He investigated the different approaches to the capacity building of DPOs in order to identify what worked, what didn't and why. It appears the relationship between Northern and Mozambican DPOs worked far more successfully than that between the latter and a more traditional British INGO. Ncube puts this down to a number of factors, including a greater level of shared experience, a willingness to give control to local people and transparency in their dealings. He offers powerful conclusions on the negative impact some INGOs have had. Questioning their role as brokers he writes that this '… relationship has short changed the disability movement, by acting as a fine sieve, which allows only minute particles to trickle down to those at the bottom. The balance of power is clearly tilted to the side of the powerful INGOs. This can be seen if we consider over the years whose capacity has been strengthened more by this relationship, the INGOs or the Southern DPOs?'

Similar questions are raised about INGOs in Chapter 11, in which the authors investigate the experience of disabled people after the Indian-Ocean tsunami of December 2004, looking particularly at how they were included in the relief effort. Although they found some evidence in India and Sri Lanka of inclusion with respect to receiving aid, disabled people's needs were not mainstreamed in relief programmes nor were they consulted at any stage. Also despite their use of the language of human rights and the social model, in practice most of the INGOs, even those that are disability specialists, continue responding to disability essentially as a question of rehabilitation. More broadly, they see INGO claims about inclusion, accessibility and support of civil society to be, '… used for the most part to give credence to agendas that are deeply destructive to the poor community as a whole, including disabled people.' Furthermore, although some aid organisations have published policies and guidelines about the inclusion of disabled people, on the ground these are either unknown or not implemented. The authors are also critical of local disability organisations, which they claim did not make common cause with other marginalised groups, but rather preferred to look for solutions with those in authority.

In the penultimate chapter, Steve Harknett offers a groundbreaking pilot study of a non-disabled led NGO working closely with disabled people in rural Cambodia. The study provides a sharp contrast to experience of disabled people with INGOs in the tsunami-effected regions. The intention was to see how to increase the role of poor, uneducated disabled people in participatory rural appraisal (PRA) methods. The results were extremely positive. They included the realisation on the part of both the NGO staff and the disabled people with the proper support, the latter could become skilled researchers. Having disabled people undertake research work in the villages also led to more positive ideas about them in the community, an important result in a country where the social exclusion of disabled people is particularly extreme. Perhaps the most salient lesson from the research, which echoes one of the most important messages from the Disability KaR is that, 'For development organisations, truly effective community development with disabled people can only be realised through promoting disabled people's participation at grass-roots level.'

Inclusive education was one of the first issues to be recognised internationally as a key development concern, not just for disabled children, but all marginalised groups. However, increasing evidence of its success and the high level international support have yet to overcome questions about its practicability and effectiveness. This is shown clearly in the final chapter in which the experiences of special, integrated (in which units of disabled children are on a mainstream site) and inclusive education programmes in four countries (South Africa, Bangladesh, Vietnam and Nepal) are compared. While each system was judged to have experienced many difficulties, overall the findings confirmed what has been observed in other countries: education at special schools was far more costly, focused on vocational, rather than academic subjects and tended to isolate disabled children from society and society from disabled children. Despite the clear financial and social benefits of a more inclusive approach to education, researchers found it was not much in evidence in the countries reviewed. For example, only in South Africa was there a comprehensive policy and action plan for educating disabled children. Although as explained by Dube in Chapter 9, there have been considerable shortcomings in delivering on these plans. But at least there is the intention of moving forward, whereas in Bangladesh the National Education Policy (2000) does not even mention disabled children.

Messages from the Disability KaR

It is impossible to do justice in this brief introduction to the very broad spectrum of issues relating to disability and development cooperation covered in this volume or what has been learned overall from the Disability KaR Programme.

Readers will have to make up their own minds. But for the authors of this introduction, both of whom have been closely engaged in the project for a number of years, the following are the five messages which stand out most significantly:

- disability is not about health status, it is about discrimination and systematic exclusion. It must be seen and addressed as a question of fundamental human rights;
- meaningful research to support sustainable development demands that disabled people and DPOs take a leading role and not simply be 'included' or 'consulted';
- development agencies themselves must set an example of good practice by drawing on the experience and expertise of DPOs in both the North and the South;
- DPOs need support which builds and sustains their capacity and not the capacity of the large corporate INGOs that all too often act as intermediaries; and
- governments and development agencies need urgently to tackle the problem of policy evaporation which has meant that good policies on mainstreaming disability in development remain almost entirely trapped on paper.

The challenge is not only to move disability up the aid agenda but to get it off the page and woven into the basic fabric of development cooperation both internationally and nationally. Our hope is that the contributions presented here will help facilitate this process.

References
Albert, B., McBride, R., Seddon, D., 2002. Perspectives on Disability, Poverty and Technology. A Report to Healthlink Worldwide and GIC Ltd. Available at: http://www.disabilitykar.net/pdfs/perspectives.pdf

Albert, B., 2004. Is disability really on the development agenda? A review of official disability policies of the major governmental and international development agencies. DKaR. Available at: http://www.disabilitykar.net/research/red_pov.html

Albert, B., Dube, Andrew K., Hossian, M., Hurst, R., 2005. Research Gap Analysis Report. Disability KaR. Available at: http://www.disabilitykar.net/research/thematic_gap.html

DKaR., 2000-2002. Website. Available at: http://www.disabilitykar.net/programme/background.html#down

DKaR., 2005a. Roundtable 2: Mainstreaming Disability in Development. Ahmedabad, India, 24 to 26 February. Available at: http://www.disabilitykar.net/roundtables/india_rt.html

DKaR., 2005b. Roundtable 3: Mainstreaming Disability in Practice: The Case of Inclusive Education. Phnom Pehn, Cambodia, 4-6 May. Available at: http://www.disabilitykar.net/roundtables/cambodia_rt.html

DKaR., 2005c. Website. Available at: http://www.disabilitykar.net/index.html

DKaR., 2004. Roundtable 1: Disability, Poverty and the Millennium Development Goals. Lilongwe, Malawi, 2-4 November. Available at: http://www.disabilitykar.net/roundtables/malawi_rt.html

DPI., 1981. *Proceedings of the First World Congress*. Singapore: 30th November – 4th December.

Hurst, Rachel., 1999. Disabled People's Organisations and Development Strategies for Change. In Emma Stone, ed. *Disability and Development. Learning from action and research on disability in the majority world*. Leeds: The Disability Press.

Ortiz, Isobel., 2004. Disability KaR: assessing connections to DFID's poverty agenda. Available at: http://www.disabilitykar.net/research/pol_assess.html

Changing the social relations of research - managing a disability research programme

Bill Albert and Mark Harrison

One of the most significant contributions of the Disability KaR centres on the research process itself and the attempt to offer a radical method of transforming the social relations of research production (Oliver 1992). The need to do this is because of the failure of international disability research in general and disability and development co-operation in particular to rise to the challenge posed by the social model of disability (see Chapter 3).

After a consideration of the way in which most research is developed and carried out, we offer an alternative method, although interestingly, one that conforms to both DFID's human rights approach to development and its Central Research Department's emphasis on research being participatory, relevant and demand led.

The traditional research model

Despite the rhetoric of the rights-based approach and the social model, most understanding of disability is still rooted in a medical or charity-model paradigm. For example, in November 2004 the Disability and Development Team at the World Bank (WB) held a meeting bringing together bank staff and outside experts on economic development to help devise a research programme on disability and poverty (Metts 2004). Reviewing notes of the meeting, there is no doubt that the discussions were informative and have given the WB a sound platform for moving ahead. However, one key element which seems to have been missing from these deliberations is the representative voices of disabled people from the South - the objects of the gathering's concern.

What was happening here, by a group with a disability consciousness higher than most and one that seems meticulously inclusive in all other respects, is a replicating of the daily experience of most disabled people – other people making decisions in their best interests. In this kind of organised 'professional' discourse, which characterises most of disability research, academics, INGOs and the entire development industry assume that disabled people are objects of concern, not initiators of such action on their own behalf. This is not to say that either the Disability and Development Team or the participants were doing anything 'wrong' or that they don't care about the lives of poor disabled people in the developing world. Far from it. It is just that they are modelling their approach to research in a way which mirrors and is likely to perpetuate the very thing they want to challenge - the social exclusion of disabled people.

Critiquing the traditional model

Of course, critiques of this kind of top-down research paradigm are well known, most prominently in the works of Paulo Freire (Freire 1972) and Robert Chambers (Chambers 1983). These are generally associated with research in the field, especially Chambers' PLA (Participatory Learning Approaches) and PRA (Participatory Rural Appraisal). However, Sue Stubbs points out (Stubbs 1999) that '..the broader philosophical and ethical issues raised in the methodology...' can be transferred to a wider research arena. She continues, 'PRA proposes a methodology which builds on the notion that local people are capable of sharing, enhancing and analysing their own knowledge in order to plan, act and promote their own development.' Further to this, Rebecca Yeo has commented (Yeo 2001),

> Traditional research often involves wealthy non-disabled outsiders questioning people about their lives. This is not a reliable way of getting information where there are big power differences and where questioners are not trusted friends. To get consent is not sufficient, as few people in situations of poverty and exclusion will refuse to be questioned by those with more power and authority. It is therefore essential that disabled people are fully involved in future research, including setting the agenda.

The main counterargument to this type of criticism is generally twofold. You don't expect other groups of people to tell statisticians, economists or other professionals such as doctors or architects how to do their jobs. Why should disabled people be privileged in this respect? Also DPOs are not likely to have the necessary expertise. In the first place, perhaps all professionals would do a better job if they listened more to those who they are supposed to serve. Disabled people would definitely put doctors and architects at the front of that particular queue. Secondly, with respect to research which concerns itself with the lives of disabled people, it is precisely these people who are the experts. If professional assistance is needed this should be put at their disposal to achieve their agenda, not the other way around. In the words of David Werner, '…it is time for non-disabled professionals to recognise the right of disabled persons to self control, and therefore to gracefully step to one side, into a role where they, as professionals, are no longer on top but rather on tap' (Werner n.d.). If disabled people are not at the very least in the room when decisions are being made about them and able to question and actively participate, then those decisions are likely to be that much poorer for their absence.

Another point frequently made is that disabled people actually are included as active participants in disability research. Increasingly, funders are demanding this as a condition for awarding disability project grants. In most cases what this has meant is that INGOs and academics, who have the resources and knowledge to bid for such grants, develop research projects and then go hunting for southern DPOs willing to become 'partners' (see below). This downstream involvement generally results in tokenism, with the research agenda being preset, the unequal power relationship between researcher and researched not being challenged and real control remaining in the hands of the intermediary organisation and/or professionals.

The foregoing arguments will be familiar to anyone who has followed the long-running debates about participatory and emancipatory research. The former is broadly about research subjects taking an active part in the process, the latter about them being able to control the process from beginning to end, thereby grounding the research in their daily experience and making it more relevant to fostering positive and sustainable change.

Emancipatory research

For disability, emancipatory research begins by conceptualising disability in social-model terms as a form of oppression, that is people with impairments having to face a complex panoply of discrimination and social exclusion. Because this involves socially imbedded discrimination and derived notions of power inequality, disability is always a political issue. Most importantly, the object of emancipatory research is to transform and emancipate, not to engage in research for its own sake. As Colin Barnes points out:

> In essence, emancipatory disability research is about the empowerment of disabled people through the transformation of the material

and social relations of research production. In contrast to traditional investigative approaches, the emancipatory disability research agenda warrants the generation and production of meaningful and accessible knowledge about the various structures—economic, political, cultural and environmental—that created and sustain the multiple deprivations encountered by the overwhelming majority of disabled people and their families. The integrating theme running through social model thinking and emancipatory disability research is its transformative aim: namely, barrier removal and the promotion of disabled people's individual and collective empowerment. From this perspective the role of the researcher is to help facilitate these goals through the research process. (Barnes 2003)

In a recent report funded by the Joseph Rowntree Foundation, *Research as empowerment?* (Hanley 2005), it was claimed that in most research with oppressed groups, because of the unequal power relationship as between researchers and researched, '…the aims or methods employed in research projects did not capture or reflect the lived experience of those it was notionally intended to benefit.' From this study a number of basic standards of good practice are put forward (see box). We feel these offer an excellent starting point for thinking about how to structure the research process so it meets the aspirations of disabled people in the South.

These aspirations came out clearly in interviews and in the response to questionnaires from all the southern DPOs (Albert, Dube, et. al. 2005). As shown below, a survey of 10 DPOs in Zimbabwe found that there was an overwhelming feeling that disabled people should have the leading role in research. In Zambia similar sentiments were expressed. The Zambia National Federation Of the Blind said that, '…disabled people should be part of the implementers of the research as this is about them and so we feel they are the best people to spell out what they want to be done.' This was echoed in replies from seven other DPOs. The country's main umbrella organisation, Zambia Federation of the Disabled (ZAFOD), observed, in line with David Werner's admonition about the appropriate roles of professionals and disabled people, that 'DPOs should play a leading role in this research process with consultancy services from research institutions.'

Good Practice in Emancipatory Research

- Users are involved from start to finish, and there is a commitment to act on the results of the research.
- Funders are equally committed to resourcing and prioritising user involvement.
- Training and support are available for users and researchers.
- A commitment to make the research accessible to those whose lives it reflects. The project does not simply end when the research is complete – there is a commitment to action as a result of the research.
- Researchers are committed to sharing power and control with service users.

(Hanley 2005)

Zimbabwe DPOs role in the research process

Response	N	%
To be on the forefront	8	90
DPs to be researchers	10	100
DPOs should take a leading role	9	90
DPOs to take an advisory role	9	90
DPs should be team leaders in research programmes	7	70

In Bangladesh a workshop was organised by the National Grass-root Disabled Federation of Bangladesh together with Action on Disability and Development (ADD) to discuss research priorities. They agreed that although capacity building and support was needed, disabled people should conduct their own research because they, 'Provide realistic information from the society and life experience, are able to find out their own problems, they know better about themselves than others…' and are well placed '…to identify ways to resolve problems.'

In Afghanistan a workshop of leaders from 12 DPOs thought that they should participate at every stage of research and that 'DPOs have experience and different ideas and views that are very important in a research process and … can provide good data from their own life experience to conduct any research on disability issue.' Many foreign agencies and some government ministries expressed roughly similar views, although it was interesting that UNICEF and Handicap International (HI) were considerably more traditional in their approach. The representative of the former said that 'DPOs should be targeted for consultation in the research work to get information from them. They can work in data collection and data processing in the research process.' The country director of HI remarked 'It is very important to listen to the DPOs as they have accurate and genuine information. DPOs will be the part of whole research process.' Clearly such approaches are more about participation, whereas here, as elsewhere, DPOs are asking for a leading role in the research process.

In this regard, it is disheartening to see that the World Bank, which should be setting the standard of best practice, is backing this kind of top-down, paternalistic approach. In a message on the Global Partnership on Disability and Development email list (June 9, 2005), in what appears to be 'business-as-usual', the WB are funding Handicap International and the Christian Blind Mission International (CBMI), another large INGO, to '...develop a framework for inclusion of disability in PRSPs.' They will, of course, 'Involve persons with disabilities in the process to help ensure that the materials correctly address disability issues', but this is very much downstream involvement, with DPOs 'participating' (and they would have to, wouldn't they?) rather than initiating or leading the process. This is, strictly speaking, a project more than research per se, but the same issues of control apply. Also, we are not decrying the involvement of such INGOs, only the dominant position of power and control they traditionally assume. It would seem that in this case the professionals are very much on top with disabled people being, as usual, on tap.

The emancipatory research process outlined above is consistent with the demands from disabled people and others in the South as well as DFIDs Central Research Department's desire '...to promote the influence of poor people and developing country institutions as potential users of research – raising the 'demand-pull' for research, so that it is more relevant.' and to engage '...users in the design, implementation and analysis of research.' (DFID 2004) Such a research structure is also in line with DFID's human rights approach to development. For example, in a DFID leaflet on human rights published in 2002 (DFID 2002), it was observed that, participation was one of the cross cutting principles upon which a human rights strategy was built. This meant, among other things '..enabling people to realise their rights to participate in, and access information relating to, the decision-making processes which affect their lives.' It was

lso pointed out that 'International Development Targets can only be achieved
arough the engagement of poor people in the development processes which
ffect their lives. The human rights approach to development means empower-
ng people to make their own decisions, rather than being the passive objects
f choices made on their behalf.' Disabled people and their families make up a
arge and disproportionate share of the poor in the developing world, and as the
revious president of the WB has said on numerous occasions, without includ-
ng them in the development agenda the MDGs will not be achieved.

Emancipatory research and the Disability KaR
The Disability KaR is an interesting case study as well as an example of the
xclusion faced by disabled people and researchers. The project began with
nly one disabled person as a research advisor. For the first year of its two-year
ife, disabled people were marginalised in and peripheral to decision making
nd programme work. What was initially seen by the disability movement as an
pportunity to develop some serious emancipatory research around disability
nd development, was never realised. At best disabled people were invited to
participate' in non-disabled researchers' agendas. If any critical comments
vere raised by the disabled adviser on plans, which were generally made with-
ut consultation, these were met with defensiveness or hostility. A view that
on-disabled 'disability professionals' expressed on more than one occasion
vas that disabled people in the North were seen to be a problem for and by
disabled people in the South. Therefore, the same professionals needed to lead
nd/or mediate programmes. This was the justification for the virtual exclusion
f disabled people from programme and decision making processes.

The problems are outlined above to show that programme was operating
n a non-emancipatory fashion. It is, however, important to state that some of
he non-disabled people involved in the programme had their own criticisms of
he approach taken and engaged in a open, critical dialogue with the disability
novement. This resulted in some very powerful alliances being forged and was
elpful in re-focussing and re-prioritising the programme.

When the original programme director resigned it was possible to open the
programme up to disabled people in the South and the North. As well as being
conscious of the power relations between disabled and non-disabled researchers
t was necessary to address questions of colonialism and ensure the programme
lid not recreate unequal and discriminatory practices between disabled people
nternationally. Because the focus of the research is on disability and poverty

in the South, it was necessary to develop transparent and open arrangements for collaborations applying the principles of 'Nothing About Us Without Us' to North-South, South-North relationships. As far as possible it was also an aim to involve disabled people as active subjects/participants in each stage of the research.

A number of things were put in place to get the Disability KaR back on track. It became possible to insert the social model as the driving approach to guide the programme. In research terms this meant making the emancipatory approach live through all the processes in the programme. This was achieved by adding additional stages to the research process. The first stage was to engage disabled people globally in deciding WHAT should be researched. This was done by initiating a consultation with disabled people in the South, both at a workshop during the Malawi Roundtable (an event organised by Healthlink International in November 2004) and with representatives of the disability movement in the North and the South through a tele-conference. The agenda setting determined the priorities for both the policy and thematic research programmes, both of which form the basis for this collection.

Once the main research themes had been agreed, the second stage was about including disabled people in a process of deciding HOW these themes should be researched and WHO should do it. This led to a research prospectus built around eight themes and priorities together with a transparent set of criteria upon which the research proposals would be judged. These were around, among other things, the involvement of disabled people as researchers, collaborations between researchers North/South and South/North and the role of disabled people in the research process. These criteria were given points against which proposals would be scored similar to what would be done at an equal-opportunity interview or in a contract compliance process:

- does the outlined method represent meaningful and genuine consultation with disabled people in the South? (10 points);
- does the outlined method allow for consultation/involvement with a wide range of disabled people, including disabled people's organisations, disabled women and people with different impairments? (10 points);
- does the research team include disabled researchers?(10 points);
- does the applicant provide evidence of capacity/track record in work of this nature? (5 points);
- does the applicant demonstrate understanding of the social model of dis-

ability? (5 points);
- does the applicant have experience of mainstreaming from other sectors? (2 points); and
- does the applicant outline a range of empowering and/or emancipatory research methods and have experience of using them? (5 points).

(Disability KaR Research prospectus 2004)

he research commissioning process then proceeded with proposals being ιdged on best quality for each theme and meeting the criteria for disabled eople's involvement. Out of the eight themes, seven research projects were ommissioned from 24 proposals. This process produced a number of high ιality submissions. It also created an exciting range of collaborations between isabled researchers, disability activists, DPO's and their non-disabled allies on ιree continents.

When Mark took over as programme director, the KaR had less than a ear to run. Because of the shortage of time the research projects had to be ompleted in 6 months. Before they were completed the research projects were resented to the Programme Advisory Group (PMG). The Research Gap Analyis, the only theme proposed by DFID, was used to inform the way forward for isability research for DFID's Central Research Department.

The final stage of the process was to invite research groups to propose ιethods of dissemination. This resulted in a wide range of user-led activities and vents including; a workshop in Malawi for the disability movement in Southern ιfrica, organised by SAFOD and FEDOMA on mainstreaming disability in deelopment co-operation, a conference ('From Policy To Practice') for national ιd regional government in South Africa, focussing on implementing disability ιolicy; and a workshop in Norway for Scandinavian DPOs and government gencies to discuss the challenges and opportunities of mainstreaming disability rought out in the research.

Emancipatory research was the preferred option because it offers the ιost appropriate methodology for understanding the socio-political process ∙f disablement – how people with impairments are disabled by the complex ιteraction of negative assumptions and attitudes about them and towards them internalised by many disabled people themselves) and a plethora of discriminaιory actions that lead to environmental, institutional and social exclusion. The)isability KaR research has demonstrated that you get better results if disabled people are in the lead or in leading roles, if necessary alongside non-disabled researchers who can act as allies. This works as long as the latter are On Tap Not On Top. It also creates sustainability, as the recommendations have a much better chance of being carried forward and implemented by disabled people and DPOs because they matter to them and because they own them. This is where the role of disability researcher and activist overlap in a positive way. The transformational power of the social action/emancipatory approach is that it understands that an informed and evidenced-based process of social change must be an integral part of the research process.

References
Albert, B., Dube, Andrew K., Hossian, M., Hurst, R., 2005. *Research Gap Analysis Report*. Disability KaR. Available at:
http://www.disabilitykar.net/research/thematic_gap.html

Barnes, Colin., (2003) 'What a Difference a Decade Makes: reflections on doing 'emancipatory' disability research' *Disability & Society*, 18 (1).

Chambers, Robert., 1983. *Rural Development: Putting the Last First*. London: Pearson Education.

DFID., 2002. *Realising human rights for poor people*. London: DFID.

DFID., 2004. *DFID Research Funding Framework 2005 – 2007*. London: DFID.

Disability KaR., 2004. Research Prospectus. unpublished

Freire, P., 1972. *Pedagogy of the Oppressed*. New York: Continuum Books

Metts, Robert., 2004. Background Paper Prepared for the Disability and Development Research Agenda Meeting, November 16. World Bank Headquarters, Washington, D.C.

Oliver, Michael., 1992. Changing the Social Relations of Research Production? *Disability, Handicap and Society* 7 (2).

Stubbs, Sue., 1999. Engaging with Difference: Soul-searching for a methodology in disability and development research. In: Stone, Emma. ed., *Disability and Development. Learning from action and research on disability in the majority world*, Leeds: Disability Press.

WCG., 2002. Washington City Group on Disability Statistics Summary Report on First Meeting, February 18-20. Available at:
http://unstats.un.org/unsd/statcom/doc02/disability.pdf

Werner, David., undated. Strengthening the Role of Disabled People in Community Based Rehabilitation Programmes. Available at:
http://www.eenet.org.uk/parents/book/werner.doc

World Bank., 2004. Summary notes of World Bank Meeting, November 16th, 2004', unpublished mss.

Yeo, Rebecca., 2001. Chronic Poverty and Disability. ADD and Chronic Poverty Research Centre. Available at:
http://www.chronicpoverty.org/pdfs/04Yeo.pdf

CHAPTER 3

The social model of disability, human rights and development cooperation

Rachel Hurst and Bill Albert

> In the last few decades, disabled people's organisations around the world have promoted a human rights approach and an environmental approach to disability issues. These approaches are both based on a social model of disability. The focus is on disabled people's rights and on the need to change society to be inclusive of everybody. Within these models, it is the way that society is organised to exclude people with impairments that is considered disabling, not the individual impairment. Organisations of disabled people have been coming together increasingly to fight for their rights on this basis. (European Union 2003)

There has been and continues to be a wide-ranging and fiercely contested debate about how disability should be understood. For those unfamiliar with this subject it might seem surprising that something apparently as obvious as the definition of disability should excite controversy. The first objective of this chapter is to outline why this has happened, why the apparently obvious is not so obvious, and why the arguments are of such importance for policies and practices concerned with disability and poverty in the developing world. This leads us to our second objective and the second half of the chapter. Here we consider why disability is a human rights issue and in turn a development issue, as well as what has been done by disabled people to put these concepts into practice.

Part 1   Understanding disability

Individual/medical model of disability
The traditional understanding of disability is that it is what 'is wrong' with disabled people – how their health is compromised. This view equates disability

with impairment. So, 'disabilities' would include blindness, deafness, the various conditions that make it difficult or impossible to walk or to speak, mental illnesses and such conditions as Downs Syndrome and epilepsy. This is a medicalised view of disability and is often called the medical model of disability.

In general, by conceptualising disability as an individual health issue, disabled people are socially imagined and may imagine themselves as, among other things, damaged, abnormal, as patients and/or as the dependent objects of a variety of medical or rehabilitative interventions. While those who view disability through a medical lens may concede that there are unfortunate social consequences that arise from having a disability, within this paradigm social exclusion is seen essentially as the result of limitations imposed by 'disabilities'. As the problem is primarily a medical one, the solution tends to be cure and/or rehabilitation. The latter, in some cases, requiring segregation into special institutions. This is carried out, usually by health service professionals of one sort or another, with the intention of caring for and protecting the disabled person, as in the case of institutionalisation, or to restore 'normal functioning'.

Social model of disability
The critique of the traditional interpretation of disability, which was eventually transformed into the social model of disability, was developed from the 1970s within the disability movement in the UK. It offered a radical alternative to the individualised medical conception of disability by asserting that disabled people were disadvantaged not because of their impairments, but as a result of the limitations imposed on them by social, cultural, economic and environmental barriers. Disability, according to this formulation, is not about health or pathology but about discrimination and social exclusion. From a social-model perspective, disability is a socio-political issue. This in turn leads to fundamentally different policy priorities and choices, mainly around the removal of disabling barriers, as well as a strong emphasis on human and civil rights.

Unlike medical model assumptions of individual abnormality and the primacy of cure, the social model, while not rejecting medical intervention, implicitly acknowledges the normality of impairment. Furthermore, it is recognised that medical advances, far from reducing the number of disabled people, have led to an increase, as people not only live longer but are also better able to survive illness and injury. It can be said that the proportion of disabled people in a population is a good indicator of an economy's prosperity.

Fierce academic and political debates continue, both within the disability movement and from outside, about the nature of the social model and its relevance, as well as how and if it can be applied in any given situation (Barnes and Mercer 2004). It is beyond the scope of this chapter even to outline these debates. Instead, after a brief account of some benefits of applying the social model in the context of development, we will consider a number of specific questions that have been raised about the social model.

The case for the social model.
By seeing impairment as an ordinary part of life, and disability as the result of discrimination and exclusion, the social model has underpinned efforts to extract disability from the medicalised, 'special needs' ghetto and push for the mainstreaming of disability concerns in all development policies and practices. Although this is yet to happen, there have been numerous positive statements of intent by both government and international agencies about the need to mainstream disability in development work (See Chapter 5).

More importantly, the social model has also provided a powerful framework for bringing disabled people together in a common struggle for equality and rights. By doing this, the social model has promoted the idea that disabled people should be actors in their own lives, rather than passive recipients of care. This equates almost exactly to current thinking on a rights-based approach to development adopted by government development agencies throughout the world and discussed more fully below.

By projecting disabled people into a leading role in defining and controlling their lives, the social model offers a powerful device for the liberation of those who remain the poorest of the poor in all countries, both developed and developing The model is so powerful because it illuminates the fact that the roots of poverty and powerlessness do not to reside in biology but in society. For most disabled people the former is immutable, while the latter, through purposeful collective action, can be transformed. As will be argued, the human rights approach offers both the platform for such societal transformation and a way for disabled people to transform their sense of who they are – from stigmatised objects of care to valued subjects of their own lives. For people who are poor and oppressed this is a key starting point of any meaningful process of social and economic change.

Relevance of the social model in developing countries
The social model has been developed in the North. Can it, therefore, be relevant

for poor disabled people in developing countries? A number of questions have been raised about the efficacy of both the human rights approach to development and the use of the social model of disability in helping to frame that approach. Some of these questions and comments on them are briefly outlined below.

Ignoring impairment?

Perhaps the most common issue raised by critics of the social model is that it ignores the reality of what impairment means for disabled people. This, they say, is problematic in the North, but when applied to the South it is catastrophic. At one level this claim could be dismissed as it is most frequently made by non-disabled people, while the social model has been embraced by disabled people, in both the North and South, who clearly do know what impairment means on a daily basis.

But more to the point, advocating the social model does not mean ignoring the causes of impairment or the health care needs of anyone, including disabled people. Proper health care is a basic human right and provision of clean water, disease prevention, ending conflicts, eradicating poverty and getting rid of landmines, all of which would remove major causes of illness and injury, are important for all. Finally, it should be stressed that the social model critique of the medical model of disability is, at least in part, about rejecting the medicalisation of disabled people, not rejecting medical intervention.

Ignoring assistive technology?

An objection related to the above point has been raised by David Werner, one of the founders of the Projimo Project in Mexico. He has written that disability activists in the North '...already have the essential personal aids they need. So their top priority is the struggle for their social rights. They have tended to project their own priorities onto the poor disabled people of the Third World, whose lack of assistive equipment (braces, wheelchairs, etc.) may be their biggest limitation.' (Werner 1998, p.6)

The issue of disability rights, far from being a Northern project, has found some of its most vocal and innovative proponents in the South. Furthermore, as the practice at Projimo indicates, access to the proper technology, far from being antithetical to a rights-based approach to disability, can be immensely liberating if developed within a framework that prioritises the real needs of disabled people, as well as their genuine participation at all levels. In fact, access to a wheelchair or a hearing aid is a basic human right for someone who would otherwise be unable to take part in social activity.

Ignoring cultural difference?

Another criticism is that the social model has been developed in the North, where the cultural context, particularly the emphasis on individual rights, differs greatly from the more family-based and/or communal situation found in many developing countries. Similar culturally-relativist arguments have been made about the international human rights agenda in general. Such criticisms raise the question of whether any practice – slavery, female circumcision, infanticide and so on – can be defended on the grounds that it is part of local culture.

More significantly, by stressing the commonality of disability discrimination, the social model, rather then promoting an individualist agenda, has helped foster cross-impairment-based collective action on issues of concern to all disabled people, i.e. transport, access to education and employment. Finally, it is up to disabled people in the South, if they find the social model useful, to interpret it in ways appropriate to their own circumstances. Such cultural adaptation is precisely what has happened in many developing countries.

Ignoring difference?

It has been claimed that the social model of disability ignores the differences among disabled people with respect to their impairments and that there is an impairment, class and gender hierarchy (wheelchair-using, middle-class men being dominant) within the disability movement (Seddon and Lang 2001).

The latter point is simply incorrect. As Hurst (2000, p.1086) has observed, '…most of the leaders of the international di/sability organisations are from the developing world, at least 40% are women and many were born in poverty and illiteracy…'. Secondly, the criticism about a lack of homogeneity is rather curious as no one has ever made such an argument or even implied that differences do not exist or are not significant individually. Disabled people, even those with the same impairment, have a vast range of life experiences, as do any other oppressed group such as women or ethnic minorities. What brings them together in a movement is the shared experience of discrimination and exclusion. This is precisely the focus given by the social model and one reason that it has been so important for, and embraced so avidly by, disabled people.

Ignoring poverty?

Why, in conditions of extreme poverty in which most disabled people in the developing world live, should they care about the social model or a rights-based approach to disability? Surely 'you cannot eat rights'. Just as surely, people without rights often can't eat. As indicated above, this latter idea firmly underpins current thinking on the poverty reduction in the developing world, with its emphasis on a human rights approach. It must be stressed, however, that this approach can only yield results for disabled people if they are able to organise and lobby effectively as equal members of civil society.

Part 2 Disability, human rights and development
In the previous section, we argued that the social-model of disability provided an analytical framework for understanding why and how discrimination occurs. Here we will show why a human-rights' approach to development offers the most effective way to address the discrimination that marginalises disabled people. We will outline what it means in practice, drawing on what disabled people have already achieved.

Human rights
Human rights are a twentieth century phenomenon developed in response to the atrocities of World War II. They set out an internationally accepted moral code by which the intrinsic humanity of every individual is recognised and protected. Human rights are the fundamental, universal and indivisible principles by which every human being can claim justice and equality.

As disability describes the barriers to achieving equality and justice which are faced by people with impairments, and because disabled people are human beings too, it is axiomatic that disability is a human rights issue. And as with all groups who face discrimination and disadvantage, it is the recognition of that intrinsic humanity that is essential to reaching outcomes that result in the full implementation and protection of human rights.

As the 24th Special Session of the UN World Summit for Social Development and Beyond (June 2000) declared, 'The ultimate goals of development are to improve living conditions for people and to empower them to participate fully in the economic, political and social arenas.' This type of development must be achieved for all people.

However, as has been repeatedly documented, access to full and equal participation has been denied disabled people in almost every country, helping to create conditions that result in them being among the poorest of the poor. At the same time, being poor is not only about being socially excluded but also makes people much more vulnerable to contracting a whole range of disabling impairments. Poverty and disability are in this sense locked in the embrace of a real dance of death. This is made far worse in developing countries in the South, where the failure of economic and social development is characterised by widespread and seemingly intractable poverty associated with wars and civil unrest, malnutrition, poor sanitation, lack of immunisation, inadequate health care, few safety provisions and pollution. Such is the music, which gives the dancers no respite.

Human rights are indivisible and universal. Continuing to leave disabled people out of mainstream systems of development, by perpetuating discrimination and exclusion, violates these rights. From a human rights perspective, development programmes can, therefore, no longer make excuses for not addressing disability, particularly as many development agencies now claim to be working within an explicit human rights framework.

A human-rights' approach to development
Since the 1990s many multi-lateral and bi-lateral agencies have adopted a human rights approach to development. This approach seeks to ensure that each person is seen as having an equal right to freedom, dignity, non-discrimination and protection from the state against abuse of these rights, together with access to economic, cultural and social rights. It is argued that only by empowering all people to be able to make decisions about their lives will it be possible to reduce poverty and achieve the Millennium Development Goals.

Universality means that all people have the right to claim agreed economic, social and cultural, civil and political entitlements. Universality also means that all people have equal rights. In practice, it is often particular groups of people who cannot claim their rights in different areas of their lives. Policies and practices of governments, civil society and the private sector may discriminate on the basis of class, gender, age, ethnicity, disability or other social status. The consequent inequities in education, health, employment, income and political representation perpetuate the powerlessness of the excluded. High levels of inequality generate social division, constrain sustainable development and are a common cause of violent conflict.

(DFID 2000)

The UK Department for International Development (DFID) has been one of the leaders in developing this approach, which was set out forcefully in white papers it produced in 1997 and 2000 and in a number of other major documents, including the 2000 target strategy paper (TSP), *Realising human rights for poor people* (Piron and Watkins 2004). While there are a great many strands to DFID's approach, the main, cross-cutting principles are:

Participation: enabling people to realise their rights to participate in, and access information relating to, the decision-making processes which affect their lives.

Inclusion: building socially inclusive societies, based on the values of equality and non-discrimination, through development which promotes all human rights for all people.

Fulfilling obligations: strengthening institutions and policies which ensure that obligations to protect and promote the realisation of all human rights are fulfilled by states and other duty bearers.

(DFID 2000, p.7)

Disabled people's role and status

Disability is a human rights issue! I repeat: disability is a human rights issue. Those of us who happen to have a disability are fed up being treated by the society and our fellow citizens as if we did not exist or as if we were aliens from outer space. We are human beings with equal value, claiming equal rights...If asked, most people, including politicians and other decision makers, agree with us. The problem is that they do not realize the consequences of this principle and they are not ready to take action accordingly. Begnt Lindqvist, UN Special Rapporteur on Disability

(Quinn and Degener 2002, p.13)

Although disabled people are mentioned in DFID's 2000 target strategy paper on poverty, the way in which their human rights are compromised and the connection between this and poverty is not spelt out. Only by understanding disability from a social model viewpoint, that is with disability being the result of systematic discrimination rather than impairment itself, can the link be made in such a way as to establish a framework for tackling the human rights abuses and poverty which characterizes the vast majority of disabled people in the South. Furthermore, as many prominent commentators have observed, unless this is done it will prove impossible to achieve the poverty reduction targets set out in the Millennium Development Goals.

As will be outlined below, disabled people have been fostering progressive social change by putting a human rights approach to development into practice, often many years before such an approach was adopted by international agencies. While DPOs are keenly aware of human rights issues and/or have explicitly adopted the social model as their guiding ideal, generally the projects and organisations have developed through a more prosaic route, people simply trying to understand the oppression they experience and struggling against it at a local or national level. As is often the case, it is only through this kind of struggle that a broader and more socially transforming understanding is achieved.

'Nothing about us without us'

It is not surprising that different local circumstances mean there is considerable variation with respect to how a human rights approach has evolved. Nonetheless, there is one defining characteristic: all such interventions based on this approach have been controlled by disabled people themselves. This in turn accords with a key observation made in DFID's target strategy paper that: 'Human rights provide a means of empowering all people to make decisions about their own lives, rather than being the passive objects of choices made on their behalf.' (DFID, 2000, p10). For disabled people this is of particular significance, since traditionally they have been seen as a group that needs to be looked after by others, not one that can act on their own behalf.

'Nothing about us without us' was the slogan promoted by Disabled Peoples' International at its founding in 1981 and has been used by disability rights activists every since. It has been particularly effective in capturing a key idea of disabled people's struggle for human rights – self determination is essential for achieving equality. This in turn has helped to unite groups from countries throughout the world in common cause. It has, for example, informed their message to governments taking part in the UN process of elaborating a convention on protecting the rights of disabled people: that in doing this they must listen to the voice of disabled people.

Disability and human rights in action

A rights based approach to disability and development is about levelling the playing field so that people with disabilities can access jobs, education, health and other services. A rights based approach is about the removal of physical and social barriers; it is about attitude adjustments for policy makers, employers, teachers, health care professionals and even family members. A rights based approach is about ensuring universal design, accessible technology, and coordinated public programmes and service. The approach requires government to provide the resources necessary to implement these goals and to enforce penalties for those who refuse to cooperate. (SAFOD 2005, p.12)

There are a considerable number of long-term projects developed by disabled people which exhibit implicitly or explicitly a human rights approach as outlined by SAFOD, as well as conforming to the DFID's three principles – participation, inclusion and fulfilling obligations – with regard to disabled people. There are local organisations of disabled people who run income-generating projects such as chicken farms or crafts, operate loan schemes for small businesses, run local community based rehabilitation services and work cooperatively with local elders to raise the status of disabled people in their village and to ensure greater access and self-determination. These groups are often linked to regional and national organisations who provide them with leadership training, capacity building and the most essential information needed to take action on these rights-based activities. It is crucial that both the local and national organisations or groups do not only take part in specific income generation or CBR projects, but are also involved in:

- ensuring that all policies and programmes that affect disabled people involve disabled people;
- raising the status and opportunities for self-determination of disabled people both locally and nationally;
- cooperating with the local community and thereby changing attitudes to

disability.

And last, but by no means least:

• Spreading the word – telling other disabled people and the wider community that disability is a human rights issue and telling them how to achieve
those rights, giving examples of good practice and how to overcome the
obstacles to inclusion and participation.

Below, two of these projects are briefly outlined in order to show how a human
rights approach grew organically out of struggles against the systemic oppression and denial of basic human rights experienced by disabled people and the
transforming power of this approach.

Self-Help Association of Paraplegics (SHAP), Soweto, South Africa

In the 1980s black disabled people in South Africa had little chance of survival
in such an inaccessible and hostile environment, let alone the chance to achieve
a decent standard of living.

In 1981 a group of eight disabled individuals, many of whom had been
disabled in the fight against apartheid and unhappy with the prospect of being
forced into institutional care, decided to set up a self help association. They
wanted to enjoy the simple dignity of being in control of their own lives but
realised this meant having to support themselves. They decided to do this by
opening a factory employing only disabled people doing sub-contract work
for industry. With start-up funding from corporations and trust funds, the first
SHAP Centre opened in 1983, the second in 1989. From the outset SHAP has
been managed by disabled people and after the initial employment initiative,
SHAP expanded its programmes to include transport, sport, education, training,
advice and peer support. By doing this it has provided a liberating example
to other self-help groups in South Africa who are, in differing circumstances,
seeking to follow their lead (Nkeli 1998).

One of the crucial elements of SHAP was its economic self-sufficiency.
After an initial injection of start-up aid funding, SHAP functioned and grew as
a non-profit making business. This has also set an example to many disabled
people's organisations, both in the South and North who, without that economic
self-sufficiency, can be constrained in their self-determination by funding criteria and the objectives of aid and development funders (DuToit 1989).

Within the context of a human rights approach, the SHAP example is
instructive because their initial motivation was about achieving economic inde-

pendence, not human rights. As Jerry Nkeli, explained:

In the early 1980s a few of our colleagues in South Africa attended an international conference organized by Rehabilitation International. The few people [from South Africa] who attended that conference were quite privileged and all were from the white community. They came back with a lot of excitement. They had the theory, they knew that it is proper to reject charity and welfare, but they didn't have the numbers. They met the self-help group in Soweto, who did not know how to philosophize, who didn't know how to contextualize their struggle, but who in a very simple way understood that they did not want charity and wanted to run their own life and who had the numbers. (Nkeli 1998)

In other words, the founders of SHAP had grasped the importance of self determination, a central element in the current human rights discourse, 20 years before it was taken up by the aid agencies. The linking of the two groups of disabled people, from Soweto and those with international experience, the example of the black liberation struggle in the US and the continuing battle against apartheid was the heady mixture out of which the South African disability movement was forged.

It is interesting to note that the same meeting of Rehabilitation International, which was to have such a strong impact on SHAP, also prompted the birth of Disabled Peoples' International. In fact, over 200 disabled people returned to their own countries after that conference and set up national organisations of disabled people whose primary demand was for 'full participation and equality in our society with equal rights and responsibilities' (DPI 1981).The leaders of SHAP went on to the leadership of Disabled Peoples' South Africa (DPSA) and then on to the world arena of disability rights, creating effective role models for disabled people everywhere.

Andhra Pradesh Rural Poverty Reduction Program (APRPRP), India
A pilot programme for reducing poverty in Andhra Pradesh, which was funded mostly by the World Bank, contained a 'disability component'. David Werner, one of the founders of the Projimo Project in Mexico, was brought in as an advisor. The work done in India bears many of the hallmarks of Projimo's participatory approach, essentially involving disabled people in leadership roles and at all stages of the process, including initial planning and the feasibility survey.

The first part of the project was extremely important, because having disabled people leading the local poverty surveys both encouraged disabled villagers to get involved and offered empowering role models. The survey was designed around a rights-based approach and drew heavily on Paulo Freire's pedagogy of liberation, based on having people describe their world and then through a grounded participatory process arrive at ways to transform it.

One of the outcomes of the survey was the setting up of disability 'sangams' (common interest self-help groups) at village level so that disabled people could work together to improve their situation, both socially and economically. In the sangams disabled people are able to define their own needs, the barriers that exist and collectively take action to overcome them. They also organise demands for legal certification (many disabled children and adults are never registered) and entitlements. Another major goal has been getting disabled children into schools, as well as obtaining the necessary medical care, surgery and assistive devices they need.

Werner writes: 'Within the self-help disability sangams in Mahabubnagar, the interest and potential exist to improve health and rehabilitation services at the village level. Such an empowerment approach could help meet an urgent need for the most vulnerable people. It would also increase respect and opportunities for disabled people. And reduce poverty.'

One of the biggest accomplishments the members say they have made is 'to be treated with respect'. 'Now people don't call us 'the lame boy' or 'the blind girl' but address us by our real names' (Werner 2002).

The disabled people who initiated this project are not yet fully involved in India's national disability rights agenda, but because of the size of the country and the cultural and political scene, the disability movement has not been able to coordinate nationally with any real coherence. They have, however, had considerable influence on the regional and local environments.

In 2003, the World Bank agreed additional support for the APRPRP with a credit of US$150 million. Judith Heumann, the World Bank's Advisor on Disability and Development, said: 'The inclusion of the disability community into this project will enable us to reach a group from the poorest of the poor, who are usually forgotten. The efforts of this project should be duplicated in other states' (World Bank Group 2003).

Conclusion

A great many more examples could be given of DPOs involved in innovative, human-rights based projects of empowerment and poverty alleviation. Most of these have undoubtedly made a considerable difference to the disabled people they have touched, the problem is that overall they have not succeeded in touching the vast majority who continue to be actively and passively excluded from the mainstream of society.

At the same time, while the social model of disability represents a protean challenge to traditional thinking about disability, neither it nor a human rights approach are magic wands. Many, including some development agencies, seem to have found the social model a helpful way to conceptualise disability. They have even begun using disability-rights language in reports and policy documents. This is not enough to make a real difference. In most cases it has only led to words substituting for action. Secondly, a too-easy acceptance of the new disability paradigm is counterproductive to the extent that, by being so easy it runs the risk of ignoring how negative assumptions and attitudes about disability (held by both disabled and non-disabled people) are so deeply ingrained and continually reinforced.

Understanding the strength and social authority of these attitudes demands a genuine awareness of the unequal power relationships that define the reality of disability. This applies equally to gender and ethnicity. For example, you cannot challenge sexism and racism in a 'white man's world' by using non-sexist, non-racist language while accepting the power relationships in that world. Until this problem is addressed and the insidious layers of institutionalised disablism are exposed and stripped away it will be impossible to develop and implement effective policies to address the disadvantage and poverty so endemic among the hundreds of millions of disabled people in the developing world.

As David Werner (2002, p.7) writes of the poverty reduction project in Andhra Pradesh:

Clearly, to substantially reduce poverty in India – or anywhere else – will require transformation of unjust socioeconomic and political structures that go far beyond the village-based health and rehabilitation measures. But in the meantime, such measures can help the most vulnerable villagers cope a bit more successfully. *By coming together to solve their problems in time a critical mass of 'people who care for one another as equals' will be reached so that, col-*

lectively, they can begin to demand and work for more far-reaching change.

Unless this happens, a human rights approach to development will be, as many critics have claimed it is, little more than empty rhetoric employed to deflect attention from the resource-draining, poverty-engendering political economy of globalisation.

References

Barnes, C. and Mercer, G. (eds.)., 2004. *Implementing the social model of disability: theory and research*, Leeds: Disability Press.

DFID., 2000. Realising human rights for poor people. London: DFID.

DPI., 1981. Proceedings of the First World Congress. Singapore: DPI Secretariat

duToit, Mike., 1989. *Self Help Association of Paraplegics, SHAP, Republic of South Africa*. Available at:
www.independentliving.org/toolsforpower/tools31.html

European Union., 2003. *Guidance note on disability and development for EU delegations and services*, EC DEV/RELEX/AIDCO and Delegations Staff Briefing Note. Available at:
www.iddc.org.uk/dis_dev/mainstreaming/guidance_note.pdf

Hurst, Rachel., 2000. To revise or not to revise. Disability and Society, 15 (7).
Lang, Raymond., 1998. A critique of the disability movement. guest editorial in *Asia Pacific Disability Rehabilitation Journal*, 9 (1).
Available at:
www.dinf.ne.jp/doc/english/asia/resource/apdrj/z13jo0100/z13jo0103.htm

Nkeli, Jerry., 1998. *How to overcome double discrimination of disabled people in South Africa*. Paper given at conference Legislation for Human Rights, Stockholm, Sweden, 24 August. Available at:
 www.independentliving.org/docs1/hr5.html

Piron, Laure-Hélène and Watkins, Francis. 2004. DFID human rights review. A review of how DFID has integrated human rights into its work. London: Overseas Development Institute.

Quinn, G. and Degener, T., eds.. 2002. Human rights and disability: The current use and future potential of United Nations human rights instruments in the context of disability, Geneva: UN. Available at: www.unhchr.ch/disability/report.htm

SAFOD., 2004. e-forum in, *Disability Dialogue*, Issue no. 4. Available at: http://216.239.59.104/search?q=cache:y0pzAgseOlEJ:safod.org/DRC/DDNo4. pdf+Disability+Dialogue+SAFOD&hl=en&ct=clnk&cd=2&client=safari

Seddon, David and Lang, Raymond with Victoria Danes., 2001. Mainstreaming disability issues into development studies – In theory and practice. Paper given at the Society for Disability Studies 14th Annual Conference. Available at: www.ee.umanitoba.ca/~kinsner/sds2001/program/sessions/sat/sa.html

Werner, David., 1998. *Nothing about us, without us: Developing innovative technologies for, by and with disabled people.* Palo Alto, HealthWrights.

Werner, David., 2002. The role of disabled persons in overcoming rural poverty in Andhra Pradesh, India' *Newsletter from the Sierra Madre* No. 48. Palo Alto: HealthWrights

World Bank Group., 2003. Andhra Pradash expands efforts to reduce rural poverty. Signing of World Bank's credit which underpins Andhra's own program of rural poverty reduction. New Delhi: World Bank. Available at: lnweb18.worldbank.org/sar/sa.nsf/0/C5CA40FB32D1DFFF85256CFD0053C A6A?OpenDocument

Mainstreaming disability in development cooperation: Lessons from gender mainstreaming

Carol Miller and Bill Albert

Disability in development remains confined, for the most part, in the 'special needs' ghetto of targeted projects concerned with health, education and welfare. Although it has been finding its way into some policy documents, in practice it remains trapped on the page, out of the mainstream – homeless (Albert 2004b). That disability finds a home is an essential first step to addressing the social exclusion and extreme poverty that affects the vast majority of the hundreds of millions of disabled people in the developing world.

One of the points that is frequently made by advocates for mainstreaming disability in development is that disability needs to be treated by both agencies and governments in developing countries as a cross cutting issue, in much the same way that gender has been. While gender mainstreaming has been used explicitly or implicitly as a template for disability mainstreaming, as far as we are aware there has been little critical engagement with the actual experience of the former in relation to the latter. This is what we hope to begin to do in what follows.

This chapter is based on a comparative desk review of two main sources of information: (1) documents outlining proposals for mainstreaming disability in multi-lateral and bi-lateral international development institutions and (2) the wide-ranging literature produced over the past decade documenting lessons and good practice in gender mainstreaming across different types of development organisations. In what follows, we distil eight lessons from the experience of gender mainstreaming which are then used to explore current strategies or proposals for mainstreaming disability in national development institutions.

We fully recognise that there are important differences between gender and disability. One of the most striking, particularly with respect to policy formulation, is the question of physical and communicative access. Besides the practical problems this can pose, it also demands that discrimination and exclusion are conceptualised in a radically different way, mainly by seeing the environment as a key discriminating and, therefore, disabling element. This in turn is based on rejecting some widely accepted ideas of normality and embracing disability as a 'normal' aspect of the human condition.

Despite these and other differences between gender and disability, the commonality of a human rights perspective and fundamental concerns about discrimination and inequality, as well as many other convergent aspects that inform both projects, make this an exciting and protean set of topics for closer investigation.

Mainstreaming to achieve equality

Although there have been a number of proposals for mainstreaming disability in development, none contain a clear, concise definition of precisely what it means. For this we must turn to gender mainstreaming. Since it was adopted in 1995 as the official global strategy for promoting gender equality there has been considerable debate about what gender mainstreaming means. Nonetheless, the following definition is widely accepted by development organisations and governments:

> Mainstreaming a gender perspective is the process of assessing the implications for women and men of any planned action, including legislation, policies and programmes, in all areas and at all levels. It is a strategy for making women's as well as men's concerns and experiences an integral dimension of the design, implementation, monitoring and evaluation of policies and programmes in all political, economic and societal spheres so that women and men benefit equally and inequality is not perpetuated. The ultimate goal is to achieve gender equality. (ECOSOC 1997)

This definition can easily apply to disability mainstreaming, is implicit in most writing on the subject and it is the working definition we use in this chapter. It is important to note that mainstreaming should not be seen as an end in itself, but rather a strategy to achieve gender or disability equality.

Disability equality is another concept that is usually not spelled out. As with mainstreaming, its meaning too is often contested. It begins with the understanding that disability is socially constructed (see Albert 2004a). This does not mean that impairments are unimportant, but only that while they can be extremely difficult for individuals, for any population they are normal. In fact, the greater the level of economic development, the more normal they become, as there is a strong positive correlation between levels of economic development and the proportion of disabled people in any population.

To achieve disability equality therefore means removing the social, cultural and environmental barriers that violate disabled peoples' basic human rights by preventing them from playing a full and equal role in society. It is important here to distinguish the social model, which is a conceptualisation of disability, from the human rights approach, which is a strategy for dealing with the discrimination and social exclusion faced by disabled people.

The strategy of gender mainstreaming was adopted in the 1990s in response to some of the pitfalls evident in earlier attempts to ensure that women were integrated into development initiatives. There is insufficient space here to explore the history of feminist activism on this front and to place it in a comparative context with the history of the disability movement. Two points are worth noting. First, isolated projects targeting women – the favoured approach to addressing gender equality – left the mainstream of development largely untouched and as such did little to challenge the power relationships and institutions through which gender inequality is perpetuated (e.g. family, household, market, state, etc.). Hence the strategy of mainstreaming described above. Second, and most importantly in this comparative context, the feminist movement had broadly won the argument that the inequality experienced by women is socially constructed, that is it has its roots in society not biology. While progress has been made, the disability movement still has to win that argument. Until it does it will continue to be difficult to convince policy makers that disability is a human rights issue and disability mainstreaming an effective strategy both to reduce poverty and achieve equality in development.

Interlocking arenas of mainstreaming
Mainstreaming in development cooperation is an intricate process that takes place across a number of distinct but interlinked realms of activity. Figure 1, borrowed from SIDA (Swhlkwyk et al. cited in Murison 2002), shows the three interconnected spheres in which mainstreaming takes place:

(1) at the level of the agency itself with respect to its culture, policies and practices;

(2) within its programmes; and

(3) the outcomes (making good on the promise of improving equality).

It has been pointed out that 'at times strategies and assessments have tended to blur these three arenas, and have often lost sight of the fact that change in the third level is the final goal... It is important not to conflate these three arenas, as different strategies and indicators of change apply to each' (Murison 2002, p.2).

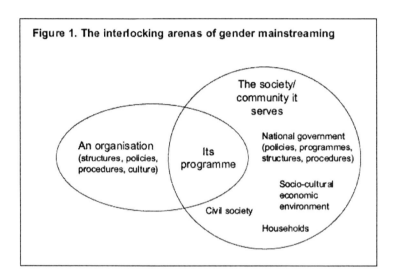

Figure 1. The interlocking arenas of gender mainstreaming

We use the schema in Figure 1 as a heuristic device to structure our analysis and tease out what those advocating disability mainstreaming can learn from the experience of gender mainstreaming.

Mainstreaming at the organisational level
The emphasis placed on mainstreaming at the organisational level (e.g. the organisational structures, procedures and culture) emerges from a long struggle to integrate gender equality issues at the programmatic level (e.g. country strategy papers, sector strategies, PRSPs, technical assistance). Evaluations have consistently drawn attention to the 'evaporation' of policy commitments to gender equality in the planning and implementation processes, as a result of inadequate management procedures and the lack of commitment, understanding and skills among staff (Derbyshire 2002).

Lesson One: the need for a clear mandate and implementation strategy on disability and development

For many development organisations, statements of commitment to disability equality are rarely backed up by an institutional policy or a clear mandate on disability. Where such policies do exist, they often remain trapped on paper.

Good practice guidelines from gender mainstreaming (see esp. Derbyshire 2002) suggest that a disability policy should:

- be a succinct statement of the organisation's commitment to disability equality;
- lay out evidence of disability inequality, drawing on relevant analytical information and disaggregated data;
- explain why disability inequality is an obstacle to the achievement of the organisation's principles and mission;
- work to address disability inequality, both within the organisation as well as externally in programme work; and
- be articulated at the highest level and communicated effectively across the organisation.

Furthermore, the experience of gender mainstreaming has shown that if the policy is taken up, subtle changes in the meaning of gender can take place which can undermine the intention of the policy (Miller and Razavi 1998; Baden and Goetz 1998). This is likely to be a more serious problem for disability, which remains, for most people, essentially a question of physical or mental deficit rather than one of discrimination and human rights. It is, therefore, necessary to monitor how key concepts are being communicated to staff and understood by them.

To avoid having the policy 'trapped on paper', a distinction should be made between a 'policy' and a 'strategy'. A strategy outlines the approach that will be used to achieve whatever goals or commitments have been made in the policy. It is a description of how the policy will be implemented. A strategy should be: time bound; specify 'Who, What, When and How?'; use clear and precise language; and be feasible and achievable. Emphasis needs to be placed on the importance of developing indicators for tracking progress and of linking regular review of the policy to other organisational monitoring and evaluation processes. These points are all relevant for disability mainstreaming.

Lesson Two: robust institutional structures to promote a disability equality agenda

While one of the tenets of mainstreaming is that 'everyone should take responsibility' for disability equality, the experience from gender mainstreaming is that unless there are dedicated structures, staff and resources, no one takes responsibility. It is now acknowledged that mainstreaming requires a twin-tracked approach, which in the case of disability mainstreaming would entail both efforts to integrate disability concerns across all programmes/sectors, as well as the need for specific disability-focused initiatives. The twin-tracked approach has implications for institutional arrangements to support mainstreaming, that is, for mechanisms to ensure that disability concerns are integrated throughout an organisation as well as for specialist disability units and/or focal points, in order to keep the issues on the agenda.

While some development organisations have recognised the need to take a twin-tracked approach to disability mainstreaming, few have developed institutional structures or appointed dedicated staff to work on disability equality issues, though there are some isolated examples (e.g. USAID, see NDC 2003).

Lesson Three: an organisational culture that is supportive of disability equality and staff that have the skills needed to mainstream disability

Over the past decade, there has been considerable emphasis on the interrelationship between internal organisational values, policies and practices and the effectiveness of external programmatic interventions in support of gender equality. Much effort has gone into identifying strategies that support organisational change (human resources policies and practices, performance management systems, gender sensitization training) as part of the overall approach to gender mainstreaming (see Macdonald 1997, p.115)

Training was one of the very first approaches used to promote gender mainstreaming and in some organisations, it has been the *only* strategy adopted. While gender training achieved much in terms of raising awareness about gender issues, its limits have also been recognised (Porter and Smyth 1997) and are likely to be of relevance to disability training as well. First, training is most effective when used as part of a broader strategy – spearheaded and monitored by staff with designated responsibility for gender issues – for influencing the climate of opinion within an organisation and promoting gender equitable practice. Secondly, there has been shift away from 'one size fits all' gender training towards more targeted training to meet specific needs, for example, general awareness raising, sector specific training, skills building on advocacy, lobbying and influencing techniques, etc. (see Derbyshire 2002). Thirdly, there is now greater understanding that gender mainstreaming involves both the need for specialist expertise as well as equipping all staff with a level of understanding, knowledge and skills appropriate to their work.

Finally, over the past decade there has been a marked tendency for gender training to be treated as primarily a *technical process*, requiring only the teaching of analytical techniques and tools. But the technocratic approach or 'winning minds' has often been at the expense of 'winning hearts' (Plantenga 2004). The lesson has been that attitudinal change about gender equality – really establishing gender equality as a core value – is crucial in fostering the level of *commitment* needed for staff to begin to build their capacity, knowledge base and skills for gender analysis and gender planning. Attitudinal change is seen as the foundation for all the other strategies to mainstream gender.

The same is true for disability but here perhaps an even more fundamental change in staff attitudes is called for because of a commonly-held, very deep-seated assumption that disability is a medical/rehabilitation problem best left to 'experts'. Although this idea is now challenged in the official pronouncements of international agencies, many of which have recast disability as a human rights issue (Albert 2004b), simply saying it does not change hearts and minds or, by extension, organisational culture. The equation is simple: the assumption that disability is about physical or mental deficit powerfully frames perception, understanding and then action. Clearly, if any issue is not correctly understood or properly identified, there is little chance of dealing with it effectively.

Interestingly, relatively little has been written about the question of organisational culture and what impact it may have on efforts to mainstream disability. An important exception is the research on British development-focused NGOs carried out by Rebecca Yeo, who observes that: 'The most significant and overriding obstacle to disability inclusion is probably a lack of awareness, knowledge and experience of disability-related issues among the staff of international development organizations...'(Yeo 2003, p.7).

The difference, identified with gender mainstreaming, between a technical approach to training and one that focuses on attitudinal change appears to have been replicated for disability (see Heinicke-Motsch and Sygall 2004), though there are examples of training that is firmly grounded in the social model of disability and taking for its starting point the need to address medically-based negative assumptions about disability and disabled people (Harris and Enfield

2003). The lesson from gender mainstreaming is that it is the latter approach that is required in order to make a real difference to organisational culture and practice.

Mainstreaming at the programme level

The shift from a focus on women specific projects to addressing gender equality within all areas of development work – one of the key objectives of a mainstreaming strategy – has required new research, skills and tools. Mainstreaming gender has involved making the linkages between gender equality and key areas of an organisation's work, from sectoral activities to poverty alleviation strategies to the MDGs. The papers exploring strategies for disability mainstreaming place considerable emphasis on the need for more research and for practical guidance and tools for mainstreaming disability at the programmatic level. We comment here on some main areas where good practice in gender mainstreaming has been identified – and address some of the ongoing challenges for taking gender and disability equality to the mainstream of development.

Lesson Four: the need for policy relevant research and information
One of the strategies of feminist advocacy targeting development institutions has been the process of identifying appropriate entry points from international, national, sectoral or organisational policy commitments to gender, to generate new research findings or analyses of sex disaggregated data. Sex-disaggregated data is statistical information on differences and inequalities between women and men: 'it is the evidence on which the case for gender mainstreaming rests' (CIDA 2000, p.32). Sex-disaggregated data provides the basis for gender analysis. Where patterns of gender difference and inequality are revealed in sex-disaggregated data, gender analysis is the process of examining why the disparities are there, whether they are a matter for concern and how they might be addressed. Good practice suggests that gender analysis should be part of routine processes of policy and project appraisal and monitoring. Gender analysis of beneficiary groups should be integral to social appraisal and monitoring processes and gender analysis of development organisations themselves should be integral to institutional appraisal and monitoring (Derbyshire 2002, p.14).

Many of these lessons may seem to be implicit in the proposals for mainstreaming disability. For example, there have been calls for the connections to be made between poverty, rights and disability and for disaggregated data 'not just according to gender, but also in relation to disability and age' (Derbyshire 2002, p.20). However, this is hardly the same as formulating a 'disability analysis' corresponding to that outlined above for gender. The other major difficulty is that there are no reliable statistics on disability. In fact, we do not even have the most basic measure – how many disabled people there are in developing countries. This is not only a question of data collection, but also, and most crucially, how disability is defined (see Albert 2004b, pp.5-7). Such a fundamental definitional issue marks a most significant difference between disability and gender, particularly when considering the ability to devise criteria for collecting disaggregated data as well as the disability equivalent to gender analysis. It is hoped that series of research projects on mainstreaming disability in development funded by DFID through the Disability KaR Programme will make a contribution to filling this gap.

The above suggests that a sound understanding of the issues to be tackled is the essential requirement for mainstreaming at the programme level, which in turn demands appropriate disaggregated data and the conceptual means (gender or disability analysis) for interpretation. This needs to be supported by action research built on the experience and expertise of women or disabled people and their respective organisations. In fact, such active involvement has been seen as one of the key aspects of a human rights approach to development.

Lesson Five: practical, relevant guidelines and tools to mainstream disability
There have been calls for more practical tools and guidelines to support disability mainstreaming. Although it should be obvious, one key lesson from gender mainstreaming is that there are 'different tools for different jobs' (CIDA 2000, p.30). Over the past decade, for example, there has been an explosion of sector-specific gender guidelines, as well as tools for gender and participation, for gender-sensitive programme cycle management, for monitoring and evaluation and for gender audits of an organisation. Despite this, practice indicates that many tools – including sector specific guidelines, manuals and handbooks – are often not being used effectively. There is greater awareness that methodologies and tools which are developed in a collaborative manner, together with those who will use them, have the best chance of being used effectively and making an impact operationally (Hannan 2004).

There are, of course, far fewer tools and guidelines for disability (see STAKES 1996 and 2000; EDF 2002; Ortiz 2004 and NORAD 2002); even for those that exist there are concerns that they are not widely known or used (see

STAKES 2003, pp.71-74 and Hertzberg and Ingstad 2004, p.18). Furthermore, as more aid is pushed into multilateral instruments, project-focused tools may become of increasingly less practical relevance. This is a problem that may be addressed, at least in part, by the use of budget analysis focused on cross-cutting issues, one of the most promising innovations over the past decades employed to support gender mainstreaming (Bridge 2003). Gender budgets are an important lobbying tool in making the national budgeting process more accountable from a gender perspective – to ensure that policy, programme and budget decisions take gender perspectives into account and that policies on gender equality are matched with adequate resource allocation. They have been used by some national-level women's networks, for example, to influence the content and processes of Poverty Reduction Strategy Papers (PRSPs). They may be a useful tool for disability mainstreaming as well.

Lesson Six: involving disabled people and disabled people's organisations at all levels
Women's participation is a key element of gender mainstreaming – it is also central to strategies being proposed for disability mainstreaming, captured in the phrase 'nothing about us without us'. The experience of gender mainstreaming suggests that it is important to be clear about the purpose of participation, consultation or inclusion. Counting the numbers of a marginalised group who have been consulted or involved in development interventions is an important starting point but cannot substitute for concrete actions to address the priorities and needs they identify. At the same time there is greater awareness of the mistakes of presenting 'women' as a homogeneous group in policy contexts when in fact different groups of women may have different needs. Intersectional analysis (see AWID 2004) is being taken up by feminist theorists and women's rights activists to examine every identity that women experience and to understand how these multiple, varied and layered identities intersect to produce discrimination and marginalisation.

Like women, disabled people are a heterogeneous group, not only in terms of having different impairments, but also across the range of identities (gender, age, race, class, income, education, religion, location, etc.). It is crucial that different voices are heard and that no section of the disability community is marginalised. However, it also must be remembered that it is generally discrimination and exclusion – the two things they share – that brings together disabled people in rights-based organisations. Finally, it is important to ensure that consultation with disabled people and disabled people's organisations happens at all stages of policy and programme development, implementation as well as monitoring and evaluation/impact assessment.

Lesson Seven: the need for 'upstreaming' disability issues in response to new aid modalities

The overall shift in official development aid towards non-project assistance in the form of sector-wide approaches (SWAps) or other forms of direct budgetary support to national governments connected to PRSPs has raised new challenges for mainstreaming. The shift to non-project development assistance increases the importance of effective policy dialogue between donors and partner governments, particularly about cross-cutting issues such as gender, which have tended to be sidelined within the new aid paradigm. Disability issues seem to have experienced a similar fate (see ILO 2002) and several guidelines have been prepared to promote the inclusion of disability issues, for example, in country negotiations/dialogue with partners (see STAKES 2003, pp.91-95; NORAD 2002; DFID 2004, pp.9-11).

While similar guidelines exist for gender, including a section on gender in the World Bank/IMF PRSP Source Book, the track record of gender mainstreaming offers a sombre picture. Current strategies adopted by gender advocates to keep gender issues on the agenda include: emphasis on supporting gender budgeting processes as well as strategies to strengthen civil society groups in pushing for policy change. The latter is one of the conclusions of a DFID disability mapping study and is something that is already being carried out by Action on Disability and Development (Thomas 2004, pp.44-48). The study's recommendations on capacity building strategies to support grassroots and other civil society organisations engaged in PRSPs may be relevant, though issues of access to political space are likely to be paramount. Overall there is an urgent need to re-examine and re-design existing policies and practices to meet the challenges of the new development paradigm and ensure that demands for gender and disability equality in development are not sidelined.

Outcomes and impact

Just as equality training or the involvement of women or disabled people and their respective organisations needs to occur in each of the three spheres of mainstreaming, so does evaluation and monitoring. We deal with it here to avoid repetition and because the subject touches most appropriately on what mainstreaming disability or gender is really about: making a positive difference to the lives and prospects of disabled people and women.

Lesson Eight: the need for appropriate tools for monitoring progress and outcomes

If we return to the SIDA schema outlined earlier (Figure 1) we are reminded that the outcomes and impact of an effective mainstreaming strategy are measured in terms of greater equality between women and men in society. Impact indicators, i.e., measuring changes in people's lives, have been among the most methodologically challenging areas of development practice, irrespective of the gender dimension.

Mainstreaming advocates are being increasingly challenged to establish the linkages between gender-related interventions (particularly institutional changes and policy) and impacts (e.g. changes in gender roles or control of resources). While this is far from being achieved in many organisations, there are some basic requirements that have been identified for strengthening evaluation and impact assessment:

- relevant baseline information;
- appropriate milestones and indicators so that progress towards greater gender equality can be identified and described;
- consultation with the community concerned to check and compare their perspectives with the information revealed by formal indicators; and
- clear reporting mechanisms that can be used to disseminate information effectively (Murison 2002, p.5).

Those championing disability mainstreaming have, for the same reasons outlined above, been concerned about monitoring and evaluation. There have been calls for the development of 'impact indicators using a human rights and social model approach to disability, integrally linked to poverty reduction indicators' along with the involvement 'of disabled persons themselves in the processes of monitoring, evaluation and research' (EDF 2002, p.25; NORAD 2002, pp.21-22; DFID 2004, p.14).

Perhaps the most promising approaches to monitoring and evaluation and impact assessment that have emerged in recent years are those that rely heavily on participatory methodologies. Such methods have been important for highlighting indicators of change in women's agency and power that would not have been identified by development planners. Since the early 1990s, and probably earlier, there have been calls for participatory evaluation of both disability projects and the disability dimension in mainstream government policies. For example, the Standard Rules include this requirement and more recently there have been detailed proposals for how self-evaluation might be structured to assess the impact of poverty alleviation measures aimed at disabled people (Nagata 2004; Rapley 2004). However, it is not clear if any of the latter ideas have been put into practice.

Conclusion

After 10 'official' years in the development arena, gender mainstreaming has generated a tremendous amount of 'heat' in the form of policies, strategies, programmes, organisational changes, research, and so on. It remains unclear, however, how much 'light', in terms of either empowerment and inclusion in the development mainstream or real, broad-based gender equality has resulted. Evidence suggests that not only do many gender mainstreaming policies remain stuck to the page, but also that as the bulk of aid has shifted into new multilateral instruments, gender concerns are being left behind. All this is not to deny that significant positive changes have taken place, particularly in such areas as education and health as well as in the lives of many women, but only that the feminist goal of fundamentally transforming the development agenda has yet to be realised. Clearly, efforts to achieve this need to be redoubled.

Those lobbying for mainstreaming disability in development can both take comfort from and be distressed by the history of gender mainstreaming. The distress comes from realising that despite the immense political weight applied to make gender a cross-cutting issue and the apparent acceptance of this by almost every development agency, the outcomes have not lived up to expectations. What chance then for disability, which has not been awarded cross-cutting status and where there is no agreement even on how to define it?

As for comfort, this is somewhat harder to find. Nonetheless, one glimmer of consolation is in understanding and accepting just how difficult it is to challenge attitudes, organisational culture and power relationships as well as to tap the financial resources and develop the commitment and skills necessary to institute progressive change. In development cooperation both gender and disability are projects which will take many years, if not decades, to realise. Those looking for 'big hits' or quick victories will invariably be disappointed. This is probably the single most important overarching lesson to derive from the experience of gender mainstreaming. The campaign will be difficult and prolonged.

In this campaign, one important advantage held by the disability movement and its allies within development agencies is the experience of gender mainstreaming: what weapons are needed, where there are pitfalls and dead ends, and the areas where breakthroughs and sustained changes are most likely.

The comparative analytical approach we have adopted has helped to highlight these issues presented in the form of eight lessons from gender mainstreaming which are of relevance to disability mainstreaming. Furthermore, it has identified some of the most significant gaps in disability mainstreaming and how these are manifest at different interconnected levels in the mainstreaming process. By doing this we have attempted to add to and/or strengthen recommendations made by others with respect to how best to mainstream disability in development cooperation.

References

AWID., 2004. Gender, Justice and Globalisation: Report on Women's Rights and Economic Change Seminar, Strategy Session, Budapest, February 5-8. Available at: http://www.awid.org/wrec.

Albert, Bill., 2004a. Briefing Note: The social model of disability, human rights and development, Disability KaR. Available at:
  http://www.disabilitykar.net/resources/karprogreports.html

Albert, Bill., 2004b. Is disability really on the development agenda? A review of official disability policies of the major governmental and international development agencies, Disability KaR. Available at:
  http://www.disabilitykar.net/resources/karprogreports.html

Baden, Sally and Goetz, Anne Marie., 1998. Who Needs [Sex] When You Can Have [Gender]? Conflicting Discourses on gender at Beijing. In: Cecile Jackson and Pearson, Ruth eds. *Feminist Visions of Development: Gender Analysis and Policy*. London: Routledge.

BRIDGE., 2003. *Cutting Edge Pack on Gender and Budgets*. Sussex: BRIDGE, IDS. Available at: www.ids.ac.uk/bridge.
CIDA., 2000. Accelerating Change: resources for gender mainstreaming.

Gatineau, Quebec: CIDA.

Derbyshire, Helen., 2002. Gender Manual: A Practical Guide for Development Policy Makers and Practitioners. London: Social Development Division, DFID.

ECOSOC., 1997. Gender Mainstreaming In The United Nations System. ECOSOC. Available at: http://www.lygus.lt/gm_en/

EDF., 2002. EDF Policy Paper: Development Cooperation and Disability. Brussels. Available at:
http://www.iddc.org.uk/dis_dev/mainstreaming/edf_policy.pdf

Hannan, Carolyn., 2004. Gender Mainstreaming: A key strategy for promoting gender equality at the national level. Presentation by Director of Division for Advancement of Women, at panel on Moving Beijing forward: Strategies and approaches for creating an enabling environment, at UN-ESCAP High-level Intergovernmental Meeting, 7-10 September. Available at:
http://www.un.org/womenwatch/daw/news/speech2004/CH-ESCAPpanelSep.pdf

Harris, Alison with Enfield, Sue., 2003. *Disability, Equality, and Human Rights. A Training Manual for Development and Humanitarian Organisations.* Oxford and London: Oxfam and ADD.

Heinicke-Motsch, Karen and Sygall, Susan., 2004. Building an Inclusive Development Community. A Manual on Including People with Disabilities in International Development Programs. MISUA.

Hertzberg, Anne and Ingstad, Benedicte., 2004. Included In Development? Report from a follow up study December 2003 – January 2004 Of the Norwegian Action Plan for Inclusion of People with Disabilities in Development Cooperation. Unpublished mss. Oslo.

ILO., 2002. Disability and Poverty Reduction Strategies: How to ensure that access of persons with disabilities to decent and productive work is part of the PRSP process. Geneva: ILO. Available at:

http://www.ilo.org/public/english/employment/skills/disability/download/
discpaper.pdf

Macdonald, Mandy et. al., 1997. Gender and Organizational Change: Bridging the gap between policy and practice. The Netherlands: Royal Tropical Institute.

Miller Carol and Razavi, Shahra., 1998. Missionaries and Mandarins: Feminist Engagement with Development Institutions. London: IT Publications.

Murison, Sarah., 2002. Elements of a Gender Mainstreaming Approach to Development: A thirteen-point framework. New York: The Capacity Development Group.

Nagata, Kay., 2004. Capacity building and technical cooperation: Disability impact assessment and disability budgeting. Paper presented at Regional Workshop on Monitoring the Implementation of the Biwako Millennium Framework for Action towards an Inclusive, Barrier-free and Rights-based Society for Persons with Disabilities in Asia and the Pacific BMF, 13-15 October. Bangkok. Available at: http://www.worldenable.net/bmf2004/slidestechcoop.htm

NORAD., 2002. The Inclusion of Disability in Norwegian Development Co-operation: Planning and monitoring for the inclusion of disability issues in mainstream development activities. Available at: http://www.norad.no/norsk/files/InklusionOfDisability.doc.

Plantenga, Dorine., 2004. Gender, identity, and diversity: learning from insights gained in transformative gender training. *Gender and Development*. 12 (1).

Porter, Fenella and Smyth, Ines., 1997. Gender Training for Development Practitioners: Only a Partial Solution. Oxford: Oxfam.

Ortiz, Isabel., 2004. Disability KaR: assessing connections to DFID's poverty agenda. Disability KaR. Available at: http://www.disabilitykar.net/resources/karprogreports.html

Rapley, Clinton E., 2004. Monitoring poverty alleviation among persons with disability. Paper given at UN ESCAP/CDPF Field Study cum Regional Workshop on Poverty Alleviation among Persons with Disabilities Lanzhou, Gansu Province, China, 25-29 October. Available at: http://www.worldenable.net/cdpf2004/slidesmonitoring.htm

STAKES., 1996; 2000. Rapid Handicap Analysis of Development Activities. An Instrument for Inclusive Project Design. In: Wiman Ronald ed.. *The Disability Dimension in Development Action. Manual on Inclusive Planning*. Helsinki: National Research and Development Centre for Welfare and Health. Available at:http://www.stakes.fi/sfa/rhachecklist%5Fkopio%281%29.htm

STAKES., 2003. Label Us Able. A pro-active evaluation of Finnish development co-operation from the disability perspective. Helsinki: National Research and Development Centre for Welfare and Health. Available at: http://global.finland.fi/evaluations/labelable.pdf.

Yeo, Rebecca., 2003. To what extent are disabled people included in international development work? How can the barriers to inclusion be overcome? A paper delivered at: Staying Poor: Chronic Poverty and Development Policy. 7th – 9th April, Manchester. Available at: http://www.devstud.org.uk/publications/reports/disability_and_development.pdf.

CHAPTER 5

Has disability been mainstreamed in development cooperation?

Bill Albert, Andrew K. Dube and Trine Cecilie Riis-Hansen

As indicated in the title of this collection and the introduction, the mainstreaming of disability in development cooperation has been the main organisational focus of the Disability KaR programme. In this chapter we summarise the findings of a research project about whether international donor agencies' policies on disability mainstreaming were being effectively implemented. If this was not happening and our initial findings suggested that it was not, we wanted to find out where in the process the policy was evaporating and how and why this was happening.

Background to the research

In recent years the mainstreaming of disability into development cooperation appears to have become a novel demand from the international disability movement and has apparently found a positive response among some international donor agencies as well as a few NGOs and INGOs (Albert 2004). However, this is far from being a new demand. Since the inception of the movement in the early 1980s, the call for inclusion and equality in all aspects of economic, political, cultural and social life has been an abiding theme. This was given an official stamp of approval in 1982 when the United Nations General Assembly adopted the World Programme of Action concerning Disabled Persons (UN 1982), in which it was stated, among other things, that, '... particular efforts should be made to integrate the disabled in the development process and that effective measures for prevention, rehabilitation and equalization of opportunities are therefore essential.' Ten years later, the UN promulgated The Standard Rules on the Equalization of Opportunities for Persons with Disabilities (UN 1993). Rules 21 and 22 provide essentially a blueprint for mainstreaming disability in development. Unfortunately, these were not binding, few resources were made available and consequently they had very little practical impact.

Nonetheless, by the late 1990s some development agencies, particularly in Scandinavia, where the disability movement had lobbied strongly for years, were making moves to develop mainstreaming policies within an explicit human rights framework (Albert 2004). At about the same time (1997) USAID formulated what appeared to be for all intents and purposes a disability mainstreaming policy (USAID 1998). In 2000 DFID published an issues paper, which many outside the department took for a commitment to mainstream disability (DFID 2000). Three years later the EU produced a detailed guidance note encouraging member states to mainstream disability (EU 2003) and in 2006 a Parliamentary Resolution was passed calling for the EU to develop an action plan to implement the note (European Parliament 2006). In 2002 the World Bank appointed a well-respected disability activist, Judy Heumann, as the Advisor on Disability and Development. This was an important move as it signaled that disability was to have a higher profile at the Bank, whose president was an outspoken disability champion.

Reflecting on the impressive catalogue of policy initiatives, of which the aforementioned were only the most prominent, it would seem that disability had finally broken through and was now firmly on the development agenda. It appears, however, on closer examination that almost none of the policies have yet to be implemented. One indication of this is that nowhere has disability been adopted as an official cross-cutting development issue. It was this disconnect between promise and action which provides the background to our research.

At the onset of our work we proposed to adopt a policy evaporation approach similar to that used in DFID for assessing the success of gender mainstreaming (Derbyshire 2002). Policy evaporation is the problem of implementation and impact failing to reflect policy commitments as policy vanishes somewhere down the organisational chain from formulation through adoption to implementation. A policy evaporation framework for assessing disability mainstreaming is critical because it allows us to identify more precisely where and why in the process problems have occurred. However, for reasons set out in the full report, carrying out a substantive policy-evaporation analysis proved impossible. Nonetheless, interviews and questionnaires with agency staff and DPOs were informed by the concept.

We also needed to be clear what we understood by 'mainstreaming'. Here we started with the following definition, adapted from gender mainstreaming (see Chapter 4). We felt it was straightforward, practical and authoritative, carrying as it does the weight of the imprimatur of the UNDP.

Mainstreaming disability into development cooperation is the process of assessing the implications for disabled people of any planned action, including legislation, policies and programmes, in all areas and at all levels. It is a strategy for making disabled people's concerns and experiences an integral dimension of the design, implementation, monitoring and evaluation of policies and programmes in all political, economic and societal spheres so that disabled people benefit equally and inequality is not perpetuated. The ultimate goal is to achieve disability equality (adapted from ECOSOC, 1997)

Most importantly, and again taking our lead from the experience of gender, we felt that mainstreaming should be seen not as an end in itself but as a strategy for building a human rights approach into development cooperation.

One of the interesting research findings is that although we felt our working definition was fairly uncontroversial, the question of what disability mainstreaming is and even whether it offers the most useful way forward for disabled people in development cooperation is contested. We will return to this briefly at the end of the report.

Research findings

USAID

In 1996 the National Council on Disability (NCD), whose members are appointed by the President to give him and the Congress advise on disability issues, published a report on foreign policy and disability (NCD 2003). In response to this, in the following year USAID produced a substantial and wide-ranging policy paper on disability together with a 'USAID Disability Plan of Action', the latter carrying the sub-title 'Mandatory Reference'. The reasons for the initiatives were the recognition that '...the needs of PWDs [people with disabilities] are the same as the needs of other constituencies with whom USAID works. Segregation of PWDs in USAID activities would tend to increase discrimination among our ranks and in the countries we serve. Consistent with our participation efforts, the Team recognized that to be effective, programs must be constructed to include PWDs at all stages of implementation.' (USAID 1998).

Of the many purposed actions was the setting up of a central disability team and the devising of disability plans by each USAID mission. The missions were also directed to make contact with local DPOs and disability training was to be provided for the entire agency.

The policy and action plan were the most comprehensive development agency instruments then available on disability. In many respects they remain so today. Not only did they recognize the need for inclusive programmes but they twinned this with the idea that national DPOs needed to be supported and engaged.

Despite these innovative plans, a series of in-house reports suggested that implementation was extremely limited (USAID 1998, 2000 and 2003) This assessment was supported by a new report from the NCD in 2003, in which it was argued that the USAID disability policy, besides being inadequately funded and ineffective, '... includes no specific objectives or timetables, creates no new initiatives to reach out to people with disabilities and does not require U.S. Missions abroad to change their practices.'(NCD 2003)

Interviews with staff at USAID confirmed that these criticisms were well founded. Although on paper it had appeared that much was being done, in fact until recently only a single member of staff had comprised the 'disability team' and she had been working part time (about 20%) on disability issues. Because no extra resources had been made available, only encouragement and advise on disability could be offered. What positive efforts that were being made seem to have come from individuals in particular missions who had an interest in disability.

Most significantly, it turns out that what appeared to be a policy was not really a policy but rather a 'policy paper', something to stimulate a dialogue in order to get people to think about and report on what they were doing on disability. It was not a genuine policy because there was no legislative mandate and, therefore, no Congressional oversight. In this case the policy evaporated at the very first stage.

Nonetheless, reading the 1997 USAID document, which is entitled 'A policy document', it is extremely difficult to fathom how this can be anything but a policy within the commonly accepted meaning of the word. That is, a set of principles or agreed objectives that staff need to be put into practice. Policy is generally assumed to set the goals of an organisation and applying it would appear to be obligatory, although exactly how it should be applied is generally the subject of interpretation and/or internal negotiation. In this instance the inclusion of an action plan together with the word 'mandatory' certainly gives the strong impression that this policy must be carried through. An organisation's stated policy also flags up to those inside and outside the organisation what it is committed to achieve and to this degree serves as the basis for holding the organisation to account. The USAID example illustrates that just indicating that something is policy may have little meaning or authority in guiding practice. As we will see, similar Alice in Wonderland problems of interpreting what is or is not policy exist in other agencies and serve to bedevil not only understanding but also cross-agency comparisons.

As in 1997, a NDC report was once again instrumental in leading to major changes at USAID. Provisions were included in the 2005 Consolidated Appropriation Act which effectively transform the 1997 'policy paper' into a mandated policy. The Administrator (director) of USAID has to ensure that all programmes and activities comply with the 1997 policy, $2.5 million was earmarked and disability advisors are to be appointed.

A spokesperson from the NDC said that they were pleased that some of their key recommendations had been taken on board. They remained concerned, however, that the amount of money and the number of staff involved would be inadequate for the task. It was also unclear how implementation was going to be monitored and evaluated. Despite these reservations, interviews suggest that overall there was optimism at the NDC, as well as at the United States International Council on Disabilities and USAID itself, that disability issues were finally set to make an impact on the agency's development agenda.

At this stage the new disability team is setting out on a different path than that traditionally used, for example in gender mainstreaming at USAID. It was felt that this often resulted in empty, 'tick-box' compliance. They also don't want to set up a separate structure as this would reinforce the impression that disability was a special question, rather than something that needed to be mainstreamed from the onset. To achieve this they want to rely on friendly persuasion rather than compulsion, by showing the various bureaus how including a disability dimension in their work will offer added value. As outlined in our report, this is similar to the tactics employed by the Disability and Development Team at the World Bank. Interestingly, at the World Bank and USAID efforts at mainstreaming, which they both refer to as 'inclusion', are mainly focused on specific sectors, countries or regions rather than the entire institution. Although this runs the risk of confining disability to its traditional realms of social welfare, education or health it is argued that this is the only alternative for relatively small, underfunded teams working in massive and generally unresponsive organisations.

It is also the case that, given the extent to which disability has hitherto been ignored, it might be seen as unrealistic to take on everything at once. The USAID team certainly feels that this is true and are anxious to develop pilot projects to demonstrate how bringing disability on board can work and deliver positive results.

What is going on at USAID at the moment is clearly a refreshing and hopeful departure. It is unique among development agencies in having a well-articulated strategy for policy implementation, a highly-motivated disability team in an advantageous position within the agency to develop that strategy and some clear procedures to take it forward. It is, of course, far too early to assess the results, but with respect to the issue of mainstreaming disability generally there are a couple of issues that need to be raised.

Nowhere in either the policy document or the draft training material is mainstreaming or a human rights approach to development mentioned. The principal words used are 'inclusion' and 'non-discrimination', both of which accord with the underlying philosophy of the Americans with Disabilities Act (ADA), the latter being an important touchstone for USAID's disability policy. We were told that 'Human rights don't fly at USAID', meaning not that they were opposed to upholding basic human rights, but that they did not follow the human rights approach adopted by UNDP, DFID or most other European development agencies. Some of this has to do with the fact that the US system is already rights based, and the government is therefore opposed to accepting any international obligations in this area. Another is that, as we were told, it is quantifiable, concrete measures of growth and development that push the meaningful buttons. As an extension of this idea it was also pointed out that the agency can only be concerned with outputs (the results of particular projects) whereas DPOs are interested in outcomes (how the outputs feed into wider social transformation).

It would require a separate essay to unravel all the many ramifications of the difference between the USAID take on mainstreaming and our initial definition that highlighted human rights and disability equality. We will return to this question after reviewing how disability is handled by other agencies. But, whether this difference is significant in terms of the impact on the lives of disabled people will have to wait until the USAID efforts have had time to be developed, rolled out and evaluated.

NORAD

In 1999 the Standing Committee on Foreign Affairs in the Norwegian Parliament declared '... that development assistance for persons with disabilities is to be given priority. The Committee refers in this connection to the need for a coherent and coordinated effort, in which the rights of persons with disabilities are included in both bilateral and multilateral assistance. The Committee stresses the need for guidelines and an overall plan to ensure that development assistance for persons with disabilities is in accordance with sound principles and principles of human rights.' (*Disability World* 2004) This was followed in the same year by the Norwegian Ministry of Foreign Affairs publishing a 'Plan for the Inclusion of Persons with Disabilities in Development Cooperation' (Norwegian MFA 1999). These developments were the outcome of a process which had begun in 1991 when the Nordic DPOs meeting in Finland decided to put pressure on their governments to include disability in their development cooperation activities. In 2000 in Copenhagen, ministers from these governments agreed to:

> Recognise and promote the UN Standard Rules as guidelines for all bilateral and multilateral development work and to assure that special measures are taken to create accessibility and participation in development society for persons with disabilities in order to strengthen their possibilities to exercise their human rights. (Copenhagen Conference 2000)

The aforementioned commitment to the Standard Rules was repeated as the overarching framework for Norway's approach to disability in development cooperation when in 2002 NORAD, working with Norwegian DPOs, produced detailed guidelines for implementing disability policy (NORAD 2002). These were firmly based around a human rights approach and a robust concept of mainstreaming.

By 2002 all the basics seemed to be in place for bringing disability fully into development cooperation. There was a policy mandated by the parliament, a written commitment drawn up by the Ministry of Foreign Affairs and detailed guidelines developed together with the Norwegian disability movement. So, what has happened?

This was essentially the main question asked in a report carried out in 2003/04 for the Ministry of Foreign Affairs and NORAD, which concentrated on Tanzania, Sri Lanka and Malawi (Hertzberg & Ingstad 2004). They write, 'A main finding of the review is that the guidelines were not known among the target group; not by the Norwegian Embassies nor by Norwegian NGOs or international NGOs that receive most support from NORAD / MFA.' It was more difficult to discover whether disability was being mainstreamed, for as the authors observe, there was considerable variation in how people understood that term. What did seem clear was that, 'Present trends in development support make it more difficult to trace how people with disabilities are mainstreamed. With sector approaches and review of PRS reforms indicators of inclusion will have to be defined.'

Our own researchers found that the embassy in Malawi was aware of disability policy but claimed that it felt its role was to encourage Norwegian NGOs to work with partners in the country. They did not, however, see it as their role to foster mainstreaming, which suggests a rather selective reading of the policy. In Zimbabwe the embassy refused to reply to our short questionnaire, saying they did not have any disability projects ongoing and also that 'They are not sure whether other NORAD offices international and regional have disability policies.' These responses support the general conclusions of the previous report. They find further confirmation in Afghanistan, where the Norwegian Embassy admitted, in an interview with colleagues engaged on another project, that the country's policy on disability was not being implemented there.

In Zambia our researcher's comments are so trenchant that they are worth citing in detail.

> It is almost signaling danger when even an officer in the information department of an agency like NORAD fails to handle a the question of a simple policy. At first I was turned away just at the reception with a clear answer that NORAD had stopped giving support to DPOs. I said fine, but what of mainstreaming programmes: I was told without a doubt that there was no such policy at NORAD when in fact I had a Policy on Disability of NORAD in my hands right there. An hour or so later I rung them, then, phones start ringing 'hold tones' until I reach this Gentleman in the inside room who agrees that they have stopped supporting directly but only helping out into the mainstream but failed to give me a concrete example of such a project...

As was the case in country, it appears that at the centre too, either there is only a vague awareness of the guidelines and policy and/ or very little is being done to make sure they are applied. For example, the Department of Quality Assurance reported that, 'Our checklists for reviews of programmes, does not include disability issues.' While the Unit for Civil Society said, 'We are supposed to ask questions on HIV/AIDS, gender and environment and assess all project proposals according to these mainstreamed issues. We are not supposed to ask questions on disability issues...' (Albert, Dube, et. al 2005).

Overall it seems that the policy and the guidelines have been given very little attention. This may be due in part to the reorganising of Norwegian development co-operation and sharing of responsibility between NORAD and the MFA. This restructuring process, which has dominated discussions and peoples' attention for the last two years, may also have served to demotivate the staff. It is obvious from day-to-day contacts with NORAD that the disability policy has been given a very low priority. Informal discussion with lower level NORAD staff also suggests that little or no information on the guidelines has been given to them by the management. Finally, based on interviews, it would seem that staff at the agency are not fully aware of the difference between disability specific programmes and mainstreaming disability, a distinction which is clearly made in the guidelines.

If disability is being afforded such a low priority at NORAD we can only suppose that at the MFA, which handles most of the development budget, it is likely to have vanished as a serious concern. This offers another reason why the NORAD/MFA study found that the guidelines were not known in the country's embassies, which come directly under the MFA.

Although of all development agencies NORAD has one of the most impressive policies on paper, that is where they have remained. This is disappointing, but offers an important object lesson – you can only judge a development agency's commitment by results, not promises. The latter are easy to make, the former much more difficult to deliver.

All the above is not to suggest that Norway is doing nothing on disability and development. In 2001 the country gave the World Bank NOK 3 million to establish a Norwegian Trust Fund for Disability and Development, which has been vital in supporting the work of the Disability and Development Team. NORAD also partially funds the Atlas Alliance, an umbrella organisation of disabled peoples organisations in Norway which manages development aid programmes. While both these moves are to be welcomed, perhaps they may also serve to make the authorities complacent about the more ambitious and

challenging job of mainstreaming disability throughout Norwegian development cooperation.

DFID

In 2000 DFID produced an issues paper entitled, 'Disability, Poverty and
Development' (DFID 2000). The main thrust of the document was that disability should be mainstreamed and twin-tracked, that is, the former should to be
complimented by disability-specific programmes where necessary. While some
outside observers thought that this represented a new policy, it didn't. In fact it
was not well known even within the organisation. A recent mapping exercise of
disability projects within DFID found that '… there is little practical evidence
that mainstreaming has taken place and disability has hardly registered at all in
the development process' (Thomas, 2004:70).

It was apparent from our discussions with DFID staff, that policy in the
department is amorphous, not easy to define or evaluate and is interpreted and
negotiated at and between all levels in the organisation. However, the one fixed
point of reference seems to be the MDGs and how these are reflected in the PSA
(Public Service Agreement).

According to our interviewees, disability does not appear in the MDG's
and therefore does not cascade down through the PSA and beyond, because of
a general lack of awareness that it is a significant issue. Due to this, disability
tends to be forgotten and has become more or less invisible, despite being recognised by such key players as the UN and the World Bank as a major issue of
social exclusion, a principal cause of poverty and something that needs to be
addressed if the MDG's are to be fulfilled.

This invisibility is part and parcel of the idea that disabled people are just
another special interest group needing only sporadic responses – as well as being
one which is particularly expensive to address. At the same time, some people
felt there was a general perception that it would be easier to move people out of
poverty who were closer to the one-dollar-a-day line than disabled people, who
tend to be the poorest. This in turn was linked to the political imperative for the
organisation of finding 'big hits' and quick results, neither of which it was felt
could be achieved by focusing on disability issues.

Finally, many of the interviewees commented on how in practice the dominance of a narrow economic focus together with an increasing concentration on
instruments such as the Poverty Reduction Strategy Papers tended to marginalise

even issues which officially had cross-cutting status, such as gender. There was generally little clear idea of what mainstreaming disability might entail in practice and a feeling that the diffuse nature of policy in DFID made it impossible to develop an effective corporate disability strategy. Looked at more broadly, there seemed to be confusion between policy (what needed to be done) and strategy (how it could be done). Within this uncertain and essentially incoherent policy framework, developing a consciousness about the importance of disability seemed to be extremely problematic.

To make this even more difficult was the point, raised by the majority of the interviewees, of the time constraints under which they all worked. Because of this, disability could be seen by many as simply one more imposition and as importantly, one which, even if they were sympathetic to the issues, they were not equipped to deal with and for which they had little institutional support. If we had had the time to dig more deeply at the other agencies, no doubt these issues would also have been flagged up.

Another issue identified was the increasing importance of PRSPs and associated aid instruments, which meant that most human rights issues, especially with respect to social and economic rights, were being ignored. This was put down partly to the emphasis on economic indicators, but also, as importantly, to the fact that disability did not appear to be a priority for most recipient countries. This was tied into what was seen as a move away from conditionality and, therefore, the inability of donors to stipulate more than the most general, high-level conditions.

The considerable degree of autonomy enjoyed by country offices was another reason given for why disability remained largely ignored, although some believed that this autonomy was positive as it meant that DFID was being responsive to local conditions and demands. Nonetheless, what appears to be an informal and disjointed policy framework which leaves so much room for interpreting how to meet the PSA, at the same time leaves little room or incentive to build disability into the picture.

While not strictly a question of policy or organisational structure, a common theme was that disability was an invisible issue, partly because there were so few disabled people working for the department. Once again, while this was not a question followed up at the USAID, the World Bank or NORAD, we would be surprised if this was not the case for them as well.

As with NORAD, DFID does not ignore disability issues and in fact, some the country offices have been active in promoting substantial disability projects

(Thomas 2004). Mainstreaming does, however, continue to be illusive, even more so because, unlike NORAD, there is no formal institutional commitment. Another interesting parallel with NORAD is the fact that DFID has a substantial Partnership Programme Agreement (PPA) with Action on Disability in Development (ADD). Unlike the Atlas Alliance, ADD is not a DPO, but it does support the work of DPOs in the South. Funding work outside the formal structure of the Department may have lead to the belief that disability was already 'being covered' by specialists and there was no urgent need to mainstream. It also suggests that, despite the Department's formal commitment to a human rights approach, by omission disability is still being left off that agenda.

Conclusions

One of our most significant findings of our study, though hardly a surprising one, is that the substantial differences in size, organisational structure, work practices as well as institutional and political culture make cross-agency comparisons problematic. For example, as we have seen, even the most basic questions of what policy is and how it is interpreted and implemented, are quite distinct in each case. This means that although there are common issues to consider, practical recommendations for mainstreaming disability in any particular agency would demand a more specific and detailed analysis.

Bearing this in mind, broad-based institutional support for disability mainstreaming has been generally weak. NORAD offers the most potent and disappointing example of this. At USAID an excellent 'policy-like' document languished for years behind a convincing façade, although fortunately it did not convince the National Council on Disabilities. And even at the World Bank, where the president has been such a vocal champion, the Disability and Development Team are having to fight to make an impression in a bean-counting culture which in practice eschews appeals to human rights (see Albert, Dube et al. 2005). The one important lesson for the disability movement to take away from this is that getting fine-sounding policies is not nearly enough. In most cases it is only a first tentative step and without continual lobbying the policies can be left swinging decoratively and uselessly in the wind.

Leaving aside what is or isn't a policy, there has been a general failure to communicate agency policies effectively. Part of this has to do with the fact that there are so many demands on agency staff that unless something is seen as an immediate priority in terms of the agency's headline policy commitments or an individual's job appraisal, it is likely to be ignored as yet another of many minority concerns such as age, children, ethnic groups, etc.. This indifference is legitimised by the fact that disability finds no explicit mention in the MDGs, is virtually orphaned in the new world of budget support and has failed to be granted official cross-cutting status by any agency.

There is perhaps a more basic reason limiting the scope of disability mainstreaming. Those campaigning for equality for women in development cooperation have yet to achieve the mainstreaming breakthrough they want, but at least they have convinced most people, especially development agency staff, that women's inequality is rooted in society, not biology. This has not happened with disability, which most people continue to see as a medical question best left to professionals. Until agency staff are given the tools to be able to view disability through a social-model lens, appeals to see it as a human rights issue that demands mainstreaming into development cooperation are likely to make little progress.

It was also clear from our interviews, especially at DFID where we spoke mainly to those without much experience of disability issues, that there is little practical guidance on how disability can be mainstreamed. The NORAD/MFA report found that the guidance note that had been provided was too complicated for those in country to use. They also observed that it had been devised for project work, not the new aid instrument regime.

Finally, given the extent of inertial resistance within agencies and governments to taking disability on board as a serious issue and the scale of the problem in terms of the numbers of disabled people in the developing world living in abject poverty, the resources, both financial and human, which are being provided to take forward the disability agenda in all the agencies are derisory.

In their report for NORAD/MFA, the authors found that there was considerable divergence in how different groups understood the concept of mainstreaming. We found much the same in our work. For most agencies it tended to be seen as a question of ensuring participation or inclusion of disabled people in specific projects, rather than at all stages of a project or across the board. So, for example, if there is a disability dimension included in an educational project, it was described as having been mainstreamed. We see this as conceptually much too narrow a reading of the process. Mainstreaming should not be just about inclusion, it must be about the precise nature of that inclusion. While, as we have indicated, it is understandable that the culture and practices of entire institutions cannot be transformed at a stroke, it is absolutely essential that the broader, more radical goals of disability mainstreaming - self-empowerment, self-determination and equality - are not soft peddled. These need to be constantly promoted and constantly revisited.

This is of central importance, for as has been demonstrated with gender (see Chapter 4), if the understanding of key concepts is diluted, even if for pragmatic reasons, the mainstreaming project can easily be sidelined and then lost. For example, Razavi and Miller have pointed out that:

'Although the gender discourse has filtered through to policy-making institutions, in the process actors have re-intrepreted the concept to suit their institutional needs. In some instances, 'gender' has been used to side-step a focus on 'women' and the radical policy implications of overcoming their dis-privilege' (Razavi and Miller, 1995:41).

There is a danger of the same thing happening in the process of institutionalising disability, where de-politicised and technocratic approaches tend to be favoured by those who either feel comfortable seeing disability as a somewhat neutral question of equal access, or don't want to rock the boat they have just managed to get invited on board. In this process, the cutting edge issues implicit in the definition of disability mainstreaming we have adapted from the UNDP, especially to do with institutional discrimination, unequal power relations (disabled people being done for and done to by others), the denial of human rights, medicalisation of disabled people, etc., can be too readily dissolved. This should not be allowed to happen. It cannot be stressed strongly enough or often enough that disability is a human rights issue and as such it is always and everywhere a political issue.

References

Albert, Bill., 2004. Is disability really on the development agenda? A review of official disability policies of the major governmental and international development agencies. Disability KaR. Available at:
www.disabilitykar.net/resources/karprogreports.html

Albert, Bill and Miller, Carol., 2005. Mainstreaming disability in development: Lessons from Gender Mainstreaming, Disability KaR, available at
http://www.disabilitykar.net/resources/karprogreports.html

Copenhagen Conference., 2000. Final Report from Copenhagen Conference

2000. Inclusion of the disability dimension in Nordic development cooperation. Available at: http://www.disability.dk/site/viewdoc.php?doc_id=195

Derbyshire, Helen., 2002. Gender manual: A practical guide for development policy makers and practitioners. London: Social Development Division. DFID. DFID., 2000. Disability, poverty and development. London: DFID. Available at: www.iddc.org.uk/info/dfid_policy.pdf

Disability World., 2004 Norway's Support for Disability and Development Projects. no. 23 April-May.

ECOSOC., 1997. *Gender mainstreaming In the United Nations system.* Available at: www.lygus.lt/gm_en/

EDF., 2002. EDF Policy Paper: Development cooperation and disability. Available at: www.iddc.org.uk/dis_dev/mainstreaming/edf_policy.pdf

European Commission, DG Development., 2003. Guidance note on disability and development for EU delegations and services. Brussels. Available at: europa.eu.int/comm/development/body/theme/human_social/docs/health/04-03_guidance_note_disability_EN.pdf

European Parliament., 2006. Joint Motion for a Resolution … on disability and development. Available at: http://www.guengl.org/upload/docs/P6_RC(2006)0031_EN.doc

Hertzberg, Anne and Ingstad, Benedicte (2004) Included In Development? Report from a follow up study December 2003 – January 2004 of the Norwegian action plan for inclusion of people with disabilities in development cooperation. Unpublished mss. Oslo.

KaR., 2004. Highlights from roundtable 1: Poverty, development and the millennium development goals, Lilongwe, Malawi, 2–4 November 2004, organised by the Federation of Disability Organisations in Malawi (FEDOMA) and Healthlink Worldwide. Available at:

www.disabilitykar.net/events/malawi.html

National Council on Disability., 2003. Foreign policy and disability: Legislative strategies and civil rights protections to ensure inclusion of people with disabilities. Available at:
www.ncd.gov/newsroom/publications/2003/foreign03.htm

NORAD., 2002. The inclusion of disability in Norwegian Development Cooperation: Planning and monitoring for the inclusion of disability issues in mainstream development activities, January. Available at:
www.norad.no/norsk/files/InklusionOfDisability.doc.

Nordic Ministers for Development Cooperation., 2001. Towards inclusion of disability aspects international development co-operation'. Communiqué, 2000 Nordic Conference on Disability and Development Cooperation. *Disability World,* Issue 6, Available at:
www.disabilityworld.org/01-02_01/news/nordic.htm

Razavi, Shahra and Miller, Carol., 1995. From WID to GAD: Conceptual shifts in the women and development discourse. UNRISD, Geneva.

Thomas, Philippa., 2004. DFID and Disability: A Mapping of the Department for International Development and Development and Disability Issues. Disability KaR. Available at:
http://www.disabilitykar.net/karreport/summer2004/mappingdfid.html

UN., 1982. World Program of Action concerning Disabled People, UN, New York Available at
http://www.un.org/esa/socdev/enable/diswpa00.htm

UN., 1993. The standard rules on the equalization of opportunities for persons with disabilities. Available at:
www.un.org/esa/socdev/enable/dissre00.htm

USAID., 1998. *First Annual Report on Implementation of the USAID Disability Policy.* Washington DC.

USAID., 2000. *Second Annual Report on Implementation of the USAID Disability Policy.* Washington DC.

USAID., 2003. *Third Report on the Implementation of the USAID Disability Policy.* Washington DC.

US Congress., 2005. Consolidated Appropriations Act, 2005. Sections 579 and 688. Washington DC.

CHAPTER 6

Disability, poverty and the 'new' development agenda

Rebecca Yeo

As has been shown in Chapter 4 (also see Albert 2004), several national and international development agencies have produced statements, guidelines and policies regarding disability in recent years. Their very existence has been widely heralded as a major breakthrough. Indeed, a common theme for many of the papers in this collection is that the mainstreaming of disability, or even its meaningful inclusion in development cooperation, is the single most important goal. But the agenda into which inclusion is sought is rarely questioned. This leads to the bizarre situation in which many other marginalised groups are campaigning against the dominant neo-liberal globalisation agenda (on which the work of the biggest financial actors in international development is based), identifying it as the root cause of poverty, inequality and environmental destruction, whilst the disability movement almost unquestioningly campaigns for inclusion within this agenda.

This chapter briefly outlines the apparent changes in approach towards both disability and poverty, the nature of the relationship between the two and considers the potential for progress through inclusion in the existing system. It is suggested that the apparently positive response by some of the bigger financial development agencies to the lobbying of disabled people is a convenient way for them to try to claim some vestiges of respect for a widely discredited international system. Some suggestions are made as to how poverty and disability might begin to be addressed more effectively, in solidarity with others tackling similar injustices.

Disability

In DFID's issues paper 'Disability, Poverty and Development' (2000), it was claimed that '...eliminating world poverty is unlikely to be achieved unless the rights and needs of people with disabilities are taken into account...Poor people with disabilities are caught in a vicious cycle of poverty and disability, each being both a cause and a consequence of the other.' (DFID 2000, p.1).

To address this problem a 'twin-track approach' was suggested; entailing 'the inclusion of...disability issues in the mainstream of development co-operation work and... direct support to organisations of disabled people and to initiatives aimed specifically at enhancing the empowerment of people with disabilities' (DFID 2000, p.11). Variations on this analysis are repeated in so many statements of international and national development agencies (see Albert, Dube and Riis Hansen 2005) as to appear to represent an undeniably true and positive approach. This chapter questions whether this analysis is indeed useful. It is suggested that poverty and disability (but not impairment) might be more usefully described as both being manifestations of the inequality on which the dominant neo-liberal agenda depends and that neither one nor the other can actually be addressed without changing this agenda.

The change in language of many development agencies has in any case not led to significant change in practice. When disability is taken into account it is mainly regarding health or welfare interventions, not in terms of equal rights of any description. Where inclusion is considered, it is within a limited framework defined by the established players. This framework is the neo-liberal agenda of free-trade and privatization, underpinned by a survival-of-the-fittest mentality. In richer countries this mentality has been softened somewhat by welfare systems, anti-discrimination legislation and assistive technology. Nonetheless, even here most disabled people live near or below the poverty line, with many relying on state benefits and charity. In poor countries disabled people face a much harder existence. The big agencies, such as the World Bank and DFID, so often quoted as responding to disability lobbyists, are deeply committed to the agenda of neo-liberalism, an agenda almost universally accepted as leading to increased inequality. Disabled people, being amongst the poorest of the poor, inevitably suffer most in these conditions. Yet when the disability movement lobbies for inclusion it is within the agendas of these agencies.

Perhaps strangest of all in the existing situation, is the widespread applause for the World Bank's statements on disability. The World Bank is not a human rights organisation, it is not concerned with equality. It encourages the taking out of loans and enforces conditions that it perceives to be consistent with building an economy able to repay the loans. Votes at the Bank are divided according to the number of shares a country holds. The economies of the largest shareholders (the US, followed by Japan, Germany, UK and France) are heavily based on the ideology of neo-liberalism and strongly uphold the interests of multi-national corporations. The poorer the country, the fewer votes it has and the less influence over the Bank's agenda.

It is therefore no surprise that the World Bank, the IMF and other international financial institutions are lead proponents of neo-liberalism. The Bank imposes free trade on markets in developing countries (while rich countries refuse to open their own), promotes privatisation of such sectors as water, electricity and health care. It is responsible for the imposition of privatised water systems in numerous countries around the world, making such basic human requirements as water financially inaccessible to many of the poorest people, whilst multi-national corporations make large profits. It is argued that by following the neo-liberal prescription, economic development will be stimulated, national income increased and poverty eventually reduced.

Reality seems to be somewhat different. Taking staple foodstuffs as just one example, Jean Ziegler (2004), UN rapporteur for food, reports that free-trade has not lead to lower market prices as was promised. Instead it has led to:

> greater inequality as a few people or corporations get rich at the expense of the majority...The same dynamic is replicated between countries and is one reason for the growing inequalities between developed and developing countries. ...The poorest and most marginal, especially rural peasant farmers, are increasingly being left behind.

It is clear who else are amongst 'the poorest and most marginal'. James Wolfensohn, former President of the Bank, made many pronouncements regarding disability, such as: 'Bringing disabled people out of the corners and back alleys of society, and empowering them to thrive in the bustling centres of national life, will do much to improve the lives of many from among the poorest of the poor around the world'. Presumably to address this, a high-profile disability activist was appointed at the Bank in 2002 to lead the Disability and Development Team (DDT).

Clearly, if at least 10% of a population are unable to contribute to an economy then it reduces economic growth and investors' ability to make profits. Some level of poverty can be seen as good for the profits (indeed an inevitable consequence) of capitalist enterprises, as it forces acceptance of low wages. However, the poorest of the poor including disabled people, are widely excluded from the economic market altogether. This causes them to be an economic burden, which is not good for profits. The level at which this is perceived as an economic problem depends, of course, on the level of their consumption of resources and the extent to which they are seen as having potential to contribute to the economy. Even the disability and development team at the Bank are clear that hard-headed economic considerations, rather than addressing disability as a human rights issue, is the Bank's primary concern (Albert, Dube and Riis Hansen 2005, p.25).

Putting aside the profit motive, the Bank's commitment to its disability and development team seems to have been only half-hearted. The impenetrable bureaucratic structure, the fact that disability has not been adopted as a 'safeguard' (World Bank speak for a cross-cutting issue) and limitations on staffing, work plans, etc. have all hampered the DDT's impact (Stienstra, Fricke, D'Aubin et. al 2002). The most telling limitation has been funding. For example, almost all the Team's financial support has had to be obtained from donations of Bank member countries. At the moment (May 2006) it seems the team is being disbanded or at least drastically reduced in size.

It might be expected that DPOs, most of which claim to be human rights' organisations, would be the first to recognise the violation of economic, social and cultural rights which have resulted from the policies of international financial institutions. A fundamental component of the Bank's strategy (as outlined below) is to be found in its structural adjustment programmes, whether of the traditional or the more modern, Poverty Reduction Strategy Paper (PRSP), variety. While these are increasingly being challenged by the anti-globalisation movement, DPOs seem to be giving them legitimacy by lobbying for inclusion within them, rather than joining other poor, marginalised people to campaign against them.

There are many possible reasons for this. Many DPOs do not in reality set their own agendas. For all the current talk of partnerships, consultation and participation, DPOs are well aware that in order to get funding they must fit in with the agendas of the big agencies. Secondly, the mainstream media pay little attention to local people's campaigning movements working outside the mainstream agenda. The media focus instead on larger organisations who have the money to pay for advertising, are easily accessible to journalists and often provide readymade media material. This makes it difficult for people to know about the scale and power of resistance in other sectors unless they specifically search for it. Furthermore, exclusion from information is an inherent aspect of the subordination of disabled people. Thirdly, DPOs have struggled so long to be recognised, that when an organisation such as the World Bank starts making pronouncements stressing the importance of disability inclusion, it would be strange not to feel a sense of success.

All these reasons may explain why the disability sector (both organisations of and for disabled people) often focuses on those perceived as having the most power, such as international financial institutions, government and bigger NGOs, rather than horizontally towards a broader-based movement of the oppressed. This phenomenon is not exclusive to the disability sector. Referring to similar lines of power in wider contexts of poverty, Hickey and Bracking (2005, p.859)describe how 'vertical linkages...preclude the emergence of more horizontal forms of collective action'. Such lack of linkages and assessment of the wider development context militates against the far-reaching changes needed to address the root causes of poverty and disablism.

Poverty

Similar to the change in rhetoric on disability there has also been change regarding the international approach to poverty reduction. There is now widespread commitment in rhetoric at least to the goal of poverty reduction and increased unanimity among the biggest actors regarding ways to achieve it.

The Millennium Development Goals (MDGs) agreed by the United Nations (2000) have been endorsed by international financial institutions, bilateral aid agencies such as DFID, as well as many NGOs. The eight Goals put the focus of poverty reduction on a wider range of issues than purely economic indicators. They are elaborated through targets and indicators linked to each of the eight goals. The task of reaching the goals is taken up by donors providing bi-lateral aid, and increasingly through the multi-lateral framework designed by the World Bank and the IMF. A key component of the IMF's Global Monitoring Review (2005) for achievement of the Goals is the dismantling of barriers to trade and encouraging private-led economic growth, in this way maintaining its usual neo-liberal approach.

Disability is not specifically mentioned in the Goals, but as Wolfensohn stated, 'Unless disabled people are brought into the development mainstream, it will be impossible to cut poverty in half by 2015 or to give every girl and boy the chance to achieve a primary education by the same date' (cited by Albert and Hurst 2005, p.5). The MDGs raise a strategic question for government agencies such as DFID: 'will the emphasis be on moving people out of poverty who are just below the poverty line, or will DFID be targeting its efforts on the poorest and most excluded?' (Thomas 2005, p.8).

In addition to the MDGs, since 1999 the World Bank and IMF have used Poverty Reduction Strategy Papers (PRSPs) as a basis for debt relief and development aid. These replaced the discredited Structural Adjustment Programmes (SAPs), which clearly emanated from Washington and had no scope for local participation or adaptation. SAPs were a set of economic reforms based on reducing government expenditure through cuts and privatisation, opening up markets to competition by ending import tariffs and subsidies to local industry. The imposition of SAPs frequently led to popular unrest as food prices rose and local producers went out of business.

PRSPs are supposed to differ from SAPs in that, according to the IMF, they are 'country-driven, based on…participatory processes for formulation and implementation' (cited by Gariyo 2002). However, as Abugre and Alexander (2000) write, 'participation in PRSPs is engineering consent for structural adjustment policies'. Just as DPOs only get funding if their needs match donor priorities, PRSPs are '…a compulsory process wherein the people with the money tell the people without the money what to do to get the money'. Although officially the PRSP process is meant to include the active participation of civil society organisations, in practice there are serious questions whether this has happened at all and where it has, if it has been anything more than a cosmetic exercise. Furthermore, as a PRSP 'represents a life-line to cash-strapped countries, a life-line that most countries cannot afford to lose' (Abugre and Alexander 2000), any demands for genuine reform are unlikely to get a sympathetic hearing.

Referring to the draft PRSP in Sri Lanka in 2002, Sarath Fernando writes, 'There's an attempt to hide the truth in the PRSP. It is clearly not intended to help the poor, but to make the country more attractive for investors,' (Christian Aid 2003). He describes how in theory, the Sri Lankan government writes the paper after wide consultation, but in practice international financial institutions such as the World Bank set the agenda. Similarly, Gloria de Silva, who led a PRSP protest group of 200 women said, 'I can't accept this as being conducive to the reduction of poverty. This is about opportunities and privileges being offered to multi-national organisations and big business ventures to invest in the country, while the people are burdened with an increasing national debt' (Christian Aid 2003).

In contrast to the participatory façade that is promoted, PRSPs are, in fact, hugely undemocratic processes whereby a government's complete agenda is sanctioned by un-elected financial institutions. Under SAPs the IMF/World Bank had power over a country's economic programme. Now approval of social and political strategy is also necessary before credit is forthcoming. Therefore, as Gariyo writes(2002, p.11), 'in most African countries there is resistance by both governments and civil society to the formulation of PRSPs.'

Perhaps most importantly, it is highly questionable whether the new aid regime can reduce poverty. According to Demba Moussa Dembele (2004),

> ... more trade and investment liberalization, more deregulation, more privatization and a further weakening of the State are more likely to generate more poverty than promote economic and social well-being. No wonder in Sub-Saharan Africa (SSA) about 500 million live on less than $2 a day, according to the World Bank. This number is projected to rise to more than 600 million in 2015, despite all the fuss about the Millennium Development Goals (MDGs).

Nonetheless, a report for the World Bank by Chen and Ravallion (2004) suggests that despite increased inequality, 390 million fewer people live on less than $1 a day in 2001 than did in 1981. They predict that by 2015 the overall poverty rate for developing countries will be just short of the MDGs. In East and South Asia the goal will be exceeded. Wolfensohn states that 'better policies have contributed to more rapid growth in developing countries' incomes than at any point since the mid-1970s. And faster growth has meant poverty reduction.' (cited by Pogge and Reddy 2005)

This assessment is highly contentious. Pogge and Reddy (2003, p.7) claim that the Bank uses an 'arbitrary international poverty line unrelated to any clear conception of poverty...employs a misleading measure of purchasing power 'equivalence' [and]...extrapolates incorrectly from limited data'. The Bank's poverty line takes account of a wide range of prices in different countries. In poorer countries, labour and services are usually cheap relative to the cost of food, whereas in richer countries services are more expensive. However, the poorest people use their income almost exclusively for basic needs such as food, water and shelter. Therefore, including comparison of other costs distorts the poverty line. Pogge and Reddy suggest poverty assessments should be based on the cost of achieving basic necessities. They claim that 'systematic distortion...may have led to an understatement of the extent of global income poverty and an incorrect inference that it has declined'.

A more comprehensive indicator strongly supports this contention. The Human Development Index (covering capabilities such as literacy, life expectancy and educational enrolment), fell in 21 countries between 1990-2003, something that was very rare until the 1980s (cited by Green and Hulme, 2005). Ziegler reports that in 1990, 20% of the world's population were suffering from extreme under-nutrition whereas by 1999 this figure had increased by 19% (2000). He also cites FAO studies indicating that the world produces more than enough food to feed the world's population. This implies that what is needed is not greater economic growth but more equal distribution of resources.

The relationship between poverty and inequality is contested. The neo-liberal position seems to be that inequality can be positive in that it concentrates capital in the hands of those likely to invest. This helps to foster economic growth, which it is assumed is necessarily positive. But economic growth does not distinguish between positive and negative transactions. Only paid work is measured, but whether this is planting trees or building bombs is immaterial. Furthermore, as Richard Wilkinson (2005) describes, the USA is the richest, most unequal country with the lowest life expectancy of the developed world. He cites how in Greece, the GDP per capita ($21,300 – CIA 2005) is half that of the USA ($40,100 – CIA 2005), whilst the life expectancy is greater (Greece 79.1 years, US 77.7 years - CIA 2005). Wilkinson goes on to report that lowest ranking London civil servants are three times more likely to die in a given year than those in the highest ranks. He concludes that inequality has a stronger effect than absolute poverty on public health.

If this is the case it makes a nonsense of focussing on the Millennium Development Goal of halving the numbers of people living on less than $1 a day, in isolation from addressing inequality.

According to a recent UN Report (UN 2004),

> The main winners of the transformation process from a state-dominated, or state- controlled, or even state-influenced economy to a liberal economy, which took place in various parts of the world, were those that happened to be in a privileged position of power or influence. Nowhere did workers, employees and small entrepreneurs succeed in modifying in their favor the national distribution of assets. Also, the much freer circulation of capital and ability to invest across national borders, combined with this privatization movement, led to a redistribution of assets from national to foreign hands.

It can be argued that the new international aid regime bears many similarities to the old regime of imperialism in which the rich and powerful imposed their will on their colonies, but now repackaged and imposed on so-called 'partners' under the name of international development. Being a partner suggests a degree of equality, but the way the current system operates is based on maintaining gross inequalities of wealth and power within and between countries. In this respect it works very well, the rich and powerful remain so and big business thrives.

Poverty and disability

Having considered some recent developments regarding approaches towards disability and towards poverty reduction, the relationship between poverty and disability will be briefly considered.

Hossain describes the poorest as 'those whom it is permissible to reject' (cited by Hickey and Bracking 2005, p.855). Dube and Charowa (2005, p.9). portray poverty as being:

> a symptom of imbedded structural imbalances, which manifest themselves in all domains of human existence. As such, poverty is highly correlated with social exclusion, marginalisation, vulnerability, powerlessness, isolation and other economic, political, social and cultural dimensions of deprivation...It results from limited or no access to basic infrastructure and services, and is further compounded by people's lack of access to land, credit, technology and institutions and to other productive assets and resources needed to ensure sustainable livelihoods

All the features sited above relate equally to disabled people. If there are such similarities between the characteristics of poverty and disability, then

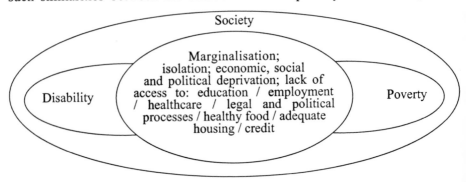

rather than the common representation of a vicious circle, perhaps the relationship would be better described as interlocking circles.

References to social exclusion are increasingly common. The logical outcome of a focus on exclusion is that inclusion is the answer, but this presupposes that the agenda in which inclusion is sought is beneficial. Bolivian indigenous organisations claiming lack of genuine representation, despite having Evo Morales, an indigenous man, as President, describe inclusion and exclusion as two sides of the same coin. Having inclusion in racist structures does not make them non-racist. Many DPOs seem to think inclusion is the answer with respect to the international development agenda. But, if it is this agenda that causes and perpetuates disability and poverty, then inclusion within it cannot be the answer.

The World Bank's report 'Voices of the Poor: Can anyone hear us?' (1999) uses interrelated circles to represent society, with poor households set apart from others. This representation is criticised by Green and Hulme (2005, p.871):

> ... it separates poverty from the rest of society, so that poverty appears as a problem of the excluded. Recommendations about getting out of poverty thus remain focused on the poor who can either increase incomes in order to access the mainstream or who can be incorporated through inclusion policies ...The problem seems to be not so much involvement in institutions per se, but rather how 'institutions' work or not to produce poverty.

Green and Hulme's observations are equally applicable to disabled people. If poor [and disabled] people are seen as 'integral to society, even if their position is marginal, it permits the perception of marginality in social terms'...poverty [and disability] can then be seen as ' ...an outcome of the social relations which tolerate, or promote, such effects.' They go further to state that '...attempts to explain poverty as a lack of something...detracts from understanding what processes are...actively creating and reproducing poverty.' (Green and Hulme 2005: 873)

In most of the chapters in this collection and the KaR programme overall, there is a strong presumption that disabled people need to be included or mainstreamed within the international development agenda. Perhaps the best example of this process in action is Dube's study of disability and the PRSP process in Uganda (Dube 2005). Here the National Union of Disabled People of Uganda (NUDIPU) put a detailed submission to those drawing up the third

Ugandan PRSP. This was based on incorporating interventions on behalf of disabled people into the existing structure. In doing this work NUDIPU built alliances with NGOs and government departments, but alliances were not built with those opposing PRSPs.

'50 Years Is Enough' is a coalition of hundreds of organisations around the world campaigning against the work of the IMF and World Bank. They criticise PRSPs for making governments more accountable to foreign donors than to their own citizens. Writing for this network, Abugre and Alexander (2000) urge people to 'rise up and demand that the institutions be stripped of their new powers to veto entire country plans.' If people en masse were to refuse to co-operate in this sham of 'participation' or the accompanying economic reforms, then governments and ultimately the World Bank would have to revise their strategies. These institutions are well aware of the power of ordinary people. Organised resistance to SAPs resulted in changing to PRSPs and attempting to make the economic reforms more politically acceptable, even if not substantially different. DPOs are being encouraged to invest more resources in submissions to this process, despite the fact that many people 'considered that the government, as well as the World Bank and the IMF, were using DPO involvement as a way of legitimising the PRSP process, rather than out of any genuine interest in the rights or needs of disabled people' (Dube 2005). This sentiment was echoed by Lugwing Miranda, the director of a disability organisation in Bolivia, who commented to the author, 'The INGOs really do nothing to help us. They only want to bring the most vulnerable people into the process of globalization'.

This point has wider relevance. George Monbiot warns that without tackling power issues, those working to 'Make Poverty History' risk giving legitimacy to the system that causes poverty (Monbiot 2005). Similarly, Hickey and Bracking refer to the 'manner in which social movements may be co-opted within regimes…as a means of securing their legitimacy rather than the objectives of the movement' (Hickey and Bracking 2005, p.859).

When the disability sector campaigns for mainstreaming in the international development agenda of organisations like the World Bank, no-one should delude themselves that the system that causes poverty or disablism will be challenged. In fact, the exact opposite is the more likely outcome.

Conclusions

Many policies, statements and manuals have been produced, regarding both disability and poverty reduction. The rhetoric has changed somewhat, but disabled people are still among the poorest of the poor and tens of thousands of people still die each day from extreme poverty. Many development agencies have done beneficial work relieving human suffering among the most disadvantaged people around the world. This can only be a good thing, unless the result is to focus resources on a particular wound, making employees and funders from the richest countries feel good about their role in its healing, but diverting attention from their role in the continual laceration of the wider body.

It would be unfair to claim that such extreme poverty is anyone's explicit intent, but it seems to be the inevitable consequence of the current system. At base there is only one cause of the daily deaths of so many poor and disabled people: inequality of resource distribution. Anything that diverts attention from this gross injustice can only be detrimental. The World Bank, DFID or any agency promoting neo-liberalism is only exacerbating this inequality. To push for inclusion within such an agenda is counterproductive to say the least.

The ideology of neo-liberalism is so prevalent as to appear to be the only game in town. This may well be intentional. Increasing recognition that the current system is causing poverty and destroying the planet has led to a growing movement for change around the world. However, what little mainstream publicity is given to anyone developing new agendas, almost universally portrays them as naïve, mad and/or dangerous. This is the case regarding the Chavez government in Venezuela, Evo Morales in Bolivia or anti-globalisation protesters throughout the world. The main threat these bring to the neo-liberal establishment is in showing that other possibilities exist. The rallying call of the Zapatistas in Mexico is not that they have the answer but that there is 'one no, and many yeses'.

It is this that the disability sector should consider. There are an infinite number of ways to structure an economic system. It should not be assumed that lobbying the most economically powerful is necessarily the most productive focus of attention.

The processes that affect disabled people are similar to those that marginalise many others. If progress is to be made, alliances are needed between these groups and their allies. Lobbying may be required in order to get disability access within other social movements. But disabled people can choose to push for alliances with the wider movement for change or get tempted by half-hearted invitations for inclusion in the very agenda that causes poverty and disables people.

The need to build alliances should not obscure the importance of the disability movement itself. It is a testament to the impact of the movement that there has been such a shift in rhetoric. The progress should be celebrated, but a modification of language, a manual or a place at the table does not indicate equal rights or justice of any kind. Pushing for inclusion without assessing the consequences could result in endorsing the system, dividing the wider movement and delaying the societal change that the social model called for many years ago.

The existing situation is not just, sustainable or inevitable. To quote from the World Social Forum, 'Another World is Possible'. It is up to us all to determine the form we would like that world to take.

References

Abugre, Charles and Alexander, Nancy., 2000. PRSP: Whitewashing Blackmail. *Economic Justice News Online*, 3 2.. Available at:
http://www.50years.org/cms/ejn/story/159

Albert, Bill., 2004. Is disability really on the development agenda? A review of official disability policies of the major governmental and international development agencies .Disability KaR. Available at:
http://www.disabilitykar.net/research/red_pov.html

Albert, Bill, Dube, Andrew K. and Riis-Hansen, Trine Cecilie., 2005. Has Disability been Mainstreamed into Development Cooperation? Disability KaR. Available at: http://www.disabilitykar.net/research/red_pov.html

Albert, Bill and Hurst, Rachel., 2005. Disability and a Human Rights Approach to Development. Disability KaR. Available at:
http://www.disabilitykar.net/research/red_pov.html

Chen, Shaohua and Ravallion, Martin., 2004., How have the worlds poorest fared since the early 1980s? Development Research Group, World Bank. Available at:
http://www.worldbank.org/research/povmonitor/MartinPapers/How_have_ the_poorest_fared_since_the_early_1980s.pdf

Christian Aid., 2003. Sri Lanka poverty strategy 'totally unacceptable', *Christian Aid News Online*. Available at:

http://www.christianaid.org.uk/news/stories/030703s.htm

Dembele, Demba Moussa., 2004. PRSPs: Poverty Reduction or Poverty Reinforcement. *Economic Justice News Online*, 7 (1). Available at: http://www.50years.org/cms/ejn/story/40

DFID., 2000. Disability, poverty and development, DFID, London.

Dube, A. K., 2005. Participation of Disabled People in the PRSP/PEAP Process in Uganda. Disability KaR. Available at: http://www.disabilitykar.net/research/small_prsp.html

Dube, Andrew K. and Charowa, Gladys., 2005. Are Disabled Peoples' voices from both south and north being heard in the development process? A Comparative analysis between the situation in South Africa, Zimbabwe and the United Kingdom. Disability KaR. Available at: http://www.disabilitykar.net/research/thematic_voices.html

50 years is enough website. Available at: http://www.50years.org

Gariyo, Zie., 2002. Participatory Poverty Reduction Strategy Papers. The PRSP process in Uganda. Uganda Debt Network Discussion Paper No.5.

Government of Sri Lanka., 2002. Regaining Sri Lanka: Vision and strategy for accelerated development draft Poverty Reduction Strategy Paper. Available at: http://www.imf.org/External/NP/prsp/2002/lka/01/120502.pdf

Green, M. and Hulme, D., 2005. From Correlates and Characteristics to Causes: Thinking about Poverty from a Chronic Poverty Perspective. *World Development,* 33 (6) pp. 867-880.

Hickey, Sam and Bracking, S., 2005. Exploring the politics of chronic poverty: from representation to a politics of justice? *World Development,* 33 (6) pp. 851-866.

IMF., 2005. The IMF and the Millennium Development Goals – a fact sheet. Available at: http://www.imf.org/external/np/exr/facts/mdg.htm

Monbiot, George., 2005. Hello Old Friends. *The Guardian*. Available at: http://www.guardian.co.uk/guardianweekly/story/0,,1528637,00.html

Pogge, Thomas and Reddy, Sanjay., 2005. How *not* to count the poor. Version 6.2. Available at: http://www.columbia.edu/~sr793/count.pdf

Pogge, Thomas and Reddy, Sanjay., 2003. Unknown, the extent, distribution and trend of global income poverty. Available at: http://www.columbia.edu/~sr793/povpop.pdf

Stienstra, D., Fricke, Y., D'Aubin, A. et al., 2002. *Inclusion and disability in World Bank activities.* Canadian Centre on Disability Studies, June. Available at: http://siteresources.worldbank.org/DISABILITY/Resources/Overview/Baseline_Assessment_Inclusion_and_Disability_in_World_Bank_Activities.pdf

Thomas, Phillippa., 2005. Disability, Poverty and the Millennium Development Goals: Relevance, Challenges and Opportunities for DFID. Disability KaR. Available at: http://www.disabilitykar.net/research/policy_DFID.html

UNDP., 1993. *Human Development Report*. New York: UN. Available at http://hdr.undp.org/reports/global/1993/en/default.cfm

United Nations., 2004. Equity Inequalities and Interdependence. International Forum for Social Development. Available at: http://www.un.org/esa/socdev/IFSD/documents/IFSDreport04.pdf.

United Nations., 2000. Millennium Declaration. Resolution 55/2 adopted by the General Assembly. September 2000 http://www.un.org/millennium/declaration/ares552e.pdf

Wilkinson, Richard., 2005. *The impact of inequality: how to make sick societies healthier*. London, Routledge.

Ziegler, Jean., 2004. Economic, Social and Cultural Rights. The Right to Food. Report submitted to the Commission on human rights. Available at: http://www.landaction.org/gallery/Zieglerpaper.pdf

CHAPTER 7

Reflections on disability data and statistics in developing countries

Arne H. Eide and Mitch E. Loeb

The principal argument for the mainstreaming of disability within development cooperation has been that poverty and disability are closely interlinked. Furthermore, because disabled people, especially women and children, comprise a large proportion of the poorest of the poor, Millennium Development Goals (MDGs) can not be met unless disability is addressed. However, because of a lack of reliable statistical data it has proved difficult to convince governments and policy makers of the real extent of disability or its functional relationship with poverty. The absence of robust figures has also made it difficult to pinpoint where intervention would be most productive, while at the same time weakening the ability of DPOs and their allies to move disability up the development agenda. This chapter addresses the current state of affairs with regard to disability statistics in low-income countries. It considers the role of disabled people themselves in the development of relevant statistics and their application, an alternative to the traditional impairment-based disability statistics, and possible ways forward to ensure that necessary data is produced and utilised for the benefit of disabled people in poor countries.

Methods

A more detailed explanation of the methodology and research activities which underpin this chapter can be found in the original report upon which it is based (Eide & Loeb 2005b). The work has its genesis in a series of studies on living conditions of disabled people in three Southern African countries (Eide et. al. 2003a; 2003b; Loeb & Eide 2004). In addition, we carried out a review of international initiatives on data collection and disability in low-income countries as well as consulting with individuals representing major stakeholders in the international development of disability statistics (World Bank, Washington City Group, UNSD, World Health Organisation). Most significantly, a workshop, including DPO representatives and researchers from the Southern Africa region, was arranged in Gaborone (Botswana) in June 2005 to address experiences and possibilities for applying research to improve the lives of disabled people.

Current initiatives to improve statistics on disability in low-income countries

UNITED NATIONS STATISTICS DIVISION (UNSD)

UNSD (2003) has published guidelines for disability statistics aimed at assisting national statistical offices and other producers of disability statistics in improving the collection, compilation and dissemination of disability data.

UNSD established the Disability Statistics Database for Microcomputers (DISTAT) in 1990 (UN 1990). DISTAT contains disability statistics from national household surveys, population censuses, and population or registration systems. DISTAT – 2 covers 179 national studies across all regions of the world. UNSD has (2003) initiated a systematic and regular collection of basic statistics on human functioning and disability by introducing a disability statistics questionnaire to the existing Demographic Yearbook data collection system (UN 2003). The information collected for DISTAT 2 covers a range of socio-economic and other variables and includes comparison with the non-disabled population. Currently however, published statistics from DISTAT – 2 refer only to the prevalence of disability by age and sex and by country. There are large differences with regards to population covered. Furthermore, statistics in DISTAT – 2 show wide variations in estimates of the prevalence. While this may be due to a number of reasons, methodological and conceptual (disability) differences are likely as major explanatory factors to this variation.

THE WASHINGTON CITY GROUP

Following an international meeting on the measurement of disability for statistical reporting in New York in 2001, UNSD authorised the formation of the Washington City Group (WG). The objectives of the WG were defined as: (1) To guide the development of a small set(s) of general disability measures, suitable for use in censuses, sample-based national surveys, or other statistical formats, which will provide necessary basic information on disability throughout the world; (2) To recommend one or more extended sets of survey items to measure disability or principles for their design, to be used as components of population surveys or as supplements to specialty surveys; and (3) To address the methodological issues associated with the measurement of disability considered most pressing by the WG participants.

The WG has also discussed various methodological issues in disability measurement, including the purposes of measurement, the International Classification of Functioning, Disability and Health (ICF) model, the UN standard disability tables, global measures of disability, the relationship of global measures to the ICF, the confounding function of assistive device use, cultural practices that influence the nature of the environment or proscribe participation, cultural issues that act as barriers to collecting data and cross-national comparability of information. A draft set of questions for the general disability measure (census questions) has been developed and is ready for testing.

It is worth noting that WG members are largely from international organisations and national statistical offices and without representation from international DPOs.

Existing data

There is little internationally comparable statistical data on the incidence, trends and distribution of impairment and disability, and much national-level data, particularly in the developing world, is unreliable and out-of-date (Moore 2003; Erb & Harris-White 2001; Yeo 2001). According to Metts (2000), internationally comparable disability statistics were virtually non-existent prior to the introduction of the International Classification of Impairments, Disabilities and Handicaps (ICIDH) (WHO 1980). ICIDH and later ICIDH-2 were designed to provide standardised disability definitions for systematic use in data collection strategies. DISTAT (1988) represents the first comprehensive attempt to identify and compile the world's existing national disability statistics (see above).

The Ten Question Screening Questionnaire (TQ) was designed by Durkin et. al. (1994) for children aged 2 – 9 years among young children in surveys of culturally diverse population, and covers six impairments ('disabilities'), including: motor, visual, hearing, speech and cognitive impairments. In some studies, TQ has been adapted to include all the under-two year olds, and it has been applied in special surveys on cognitive impairments (Islam, Durkin & Zaman 1993). It has been applied in large and comparable prevalence studies in a number of low-income countries (for detailed references see, Eide and Loeb 2005b)

Most low-income countries carry out population censuses at regular intervals. Some of these censuses have also included questions to map the number of individuals with different types of impairments. While this forms the basis for DISTAT, the information value is limited and often based on outdated screening questions. This situation will improve following agreement on global standard questions for censuses.

There are examples of national studies with more comprehensive information on disability. One example is the Level of Living Survey in Namibia (NPC 2000), that produced some, although limited, information on differences in standard of living between disabled and non-disabled people. Another example is the CASE study in South Africa (Schneider et. al. 1999) that was carried out to determine the prevalence of disabilities (impairments) as well as to describe the disability experience as reported by disabled people. A third example is the Census 2001 in South Africa (SSA 2001) that not only attempted to apply an activity-based screening question, but also included questions on standard of living, yielding some possibilities for comparison between disabled and non-disabled people.

Yeo & Moore (2003) present a convincing picture of the close link between poverty and disability. The authors present a theoretical model that is supported by the literature, showing that chronic poverty can lead to higher risk of illness, accidents and impairment, while impairments can lead to poverty and exclusion. The authors also refer to a number of sources which taken together strongly indicate that disabled people are poorer than their non-disabled counterparts. Yeo and Moore, referring to Erb & Harriss-White (2001) rightly say that, 'Despite the obvious relationships between impairment, disability and poverty, there is little internationally comparable statistical data on the incidence, trends and distribution of impairment and disability, and much national-level data is unreliable and out-of-date'. An exception is found in the SIDA report on Poverty and Disability (SIDA 1995), based on data from a multi-country study in Asia and Africa.

Because little basic research appears to have been done on poverty and disability in developing countries, Elwan (1999) recommends further investigation in several areas, including: search for additional data sources and existing analysis to allow more detailed examination of poverty-related factors, such as income, education, employment, access to services, etc; modelling of potential 'poverty paths' in populations that have a particular disability pattern, a special vulnerability, or are at particular risk of poverty; longer-term studies of income and other poverty indicators, using consistent data sets over at least two points of time, where changes in status can be observed; focused studies of gender, disability and poverty and validation of measures of disability.

Recently, a database on living conditions among disabled people in Southern Africa has been established and is gradually being built up. These national and representative studies started in 1989, today cover Namibia, Zimbabwe and Malawi and will be further expanded to Zambia (2005-2006) and Mozambique (2006 – 2008). The studies form a core element in the strategic collaboration between SAFOD (Southern African Federation of the Disabled) and the Norwegian Federation of Organisations of Disabled People (FFO), with SINTEF Health Research as the responsible research institute. The role of disabled people's organisations (DPOs) in this research has been unique in that they have initiated the program. This has meant that they have taken a lead role, with DPOs having been in control of all stages of the research process.

Furthermore, disabled people have been involved as supervisors, enumerators, members of references groups, participants at capacity building programmes, as well as in dissemination and the application of results.

The studies in Southern Africa are the first generation of studies including a large number of indicators on living conditions and disability-specific data. They are also the first which allow for a broad comparison between disabled and non-disabled people (at the individual and household level) within and across different contexts (region, countries, urban/rural). Moreover, the studies represent an attempt at utilising core components of the ICF (WHO 2001) both in the identification of individuals and in the analyses.

Application of disability statistics

A workshop including DPO representatives and researchers from the region was arranged in Gaborone (Botswana) in June 2005 to discuss experiences with applying the data from the studies on living conditions among disabled people in Southern Africa. Detailed examples can be found in the full version of this report. (Eide & Loeb 2005b) The following are the main conclusions from the workshop.

i) Anchoring and ownership of research are fundamental issues that will ensure its subsequent application in the region. As the current research on living conditions is DPO-commissioned and initiated, this also implies that the main responsibility for utilising the results lies with the DPOs themselves. Experiences from the Namibian survey of living conditions further indicate that DPO-initiated research risks being underutilised by the government. Governments in the region may be more or less involved in this research and thus more or less inclined to use it. The message is, however, that DPO-initiated research will have to be followed up by DPOs themselves if they want to achieve tangible results.

ii) An important lesson learned from the studies on living conditions in the region is that it is not sufficient to increase capacity among DPOs in order to develop fruitful collaboration with DPOs. Just as important is capacity building in participatory research among researchers and research institutes. A working relationship between DPOs and researchers that is conducive to high quality and useful outputs is crucial. Without researchers taking this seriously and, in fact, giving control of research as much as possible to DPOs, collaboration will fail and further cement a tradition of patronising, top-down, frequently negative relationships between DPOs and academic institutions. Researchers need to acknowledge the rights of disabled people and the practical consequences of these rights with regards to research. Participatory research in general and with DPOs and disabled people in particular, is in many ways a sub-discipline in research, with its own skills and rules.

iii) It is of great importance that DPOs establish and develop a strategic rela-tionship with the authorities, both political and bureaucratic, in their respective countries. Examples from both Malawi and Zimbabwe have shown that being in a good position in this regard results in having influence, and research on living conditions provides that influence with content. This in turn is highly effective and helps ensure that the application of this research has the best outcome for disabled people. DPO leadership should be advised to choose this as an arena for capacity building and act strategically with regards to both national and regional authorities.

iv) Mainstreaming research on disability was discussed at the workshop in con-nection with this study. Examples presented at the workshop have shown, for instance in Zimbabwe, that the comparative perspective in the current studies on living conditions is a powerful tool in the development of all policies and service provision. The studies on living conditions among disabled people in Southern Africa demonstrate clearly that individuals are worse off than non-disabled on a number of indicators of welfare and living conditions such as employment, education, and income. Such hard data can be used to argue that this situation is not acceptable. This is particularly the case in countries with a national policy on disability. More generally, such information is useful in lobbying governments to live up to their obligations under the Standard Rules on the Equalisation of Opportunities for Persons with Disabilities (UN 1994) as well as what they need to do in order to address poverty-reduction targets set out in the Millennium Development Goals. The issue of disability and the unacceptable differences between groups of people is relevant across sectors and disciplines. In this way, disability may be applied as a cross-cutting issue and thus contribute to a fairer distribution of benefits and services.

v) A grass-roots strategy for research was particularly called for during the workshop. This has several aspects, including DPO control of research, contextual and cultural adaptation as well as involvement of disabled people in the research process. Added to these are; objectives of research being in accordance with DPO priorities, ensuring feedback to disabled people, explicit, binding and measurable components dealing with application of research and long-term capacity building among DPOs.

Impairment based vs. activity based measures
It is difficult to detach the issue of disability prevalence from an impairment-based approach to disability, i.e. the possibility of distinguishing between disabled and non-disabled sub-populations by means of a standard procedure for screening. In certain circumstances this approach is justified. Sometimes it is important to 'count' impairment as a proxy for disability in a population. Politicians can only argue for the provision and distribution of resources based on reliable information on the proportion of the population that need these resources. Disability benefits can only be provided to those who have demonstrated that they are in fact disabled. Similarly, at the service delivery level, the equitable delivery of services must be based on the need manifested in the community. Also, comparison between individuals both with and without impairments can be a powerful tool in improving standards of living among those who have less.

Any standardised screening procedure is bound to be culturally and contextually biased and will consequently produce figures that are confounded by cultural, contextual, and environmental factors. Much can be done by standardising measurement globally, although a requirement will be that this is underpinned

globally by the continued convergence in the conceptual understanding of disability. ICF is a ready vehicle in this case.

An alternative to the medically-based dichotomisation into disabled and
non-disabled is to regard disability as a continuum.

Figure 1. Activity limitation as a continuum

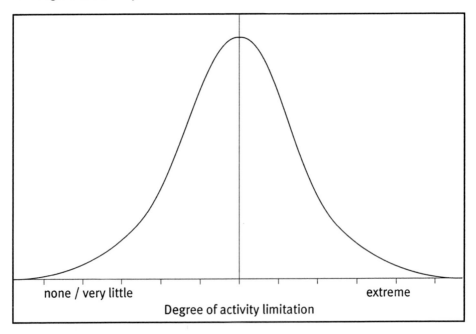

Figure 1 shows a theoretical distribution of activity limitation in a population. Activity limitation is here seen as a continuum from none/very little to
extreme. Such a functional representation of disability (activity limitation) in a
population will necessarily be more skewed than normal - hence the 'floating'
vertical dashed line. The theory behind this representation is that every individual in a population will find themselves somewhere along this distribution.
All of those with impairments will not necessarily find themselves above the
mean, for example; nor will all those seen as non-disabled be located below the
mean. Individuals with the same impairments have different needs and score
differently on degree of activity limitation.

Understood and applied in this way, we are in reality dealing with a different phenomenon, quite detached from a root, medical condition (impairment

and diagnosis). Activity limitations (and restrictions in social participation) may thus be regarded as universal phenomena that are relevant to everyone regardless of health condition. It is possible to score on the activity limitation scale without having any chronic health condition or impairment and it is possible for someone with a health condition or an impairment to score zero or very low.

Although almost every study on disability and poverty strongly suggests a high correlation between these variables, both in the North and the South, better quality statistics are still necessary. These are required not only to demonstrate in an empirical fashion that disabled people are among the most disadvantaged, but also to produce a more precise understanding about the disability – poverty relationship. At the moment, policy makers attempting to design and implement more inclusive disability policies are hampered because of meagre information, inadequate data and hardly any coordination of activities. This applies to disability policies everywhere, but the situation is worse in low-income countries. Although there are specific problems related to disability statistics in the latter, standardisation and comparability of disability statistics clearly needs to be resolved at a global level. The work carried out by the Washington City Group is in this regard of great importance to the extent that it is adopted and applied across the world.

We argue that dividing the population into disabled and non-disabled although useful for many purposes, is also problematic and probably contributes to reinforcing negative stereotypes. An alternative way of measuring 'disability' is to draw on the ICF model and apply 'activity limitation' (and/or likewise 'restrictions in social participation') as an indicator of a general phenomenon that applies to anyone regardless of health and impairment status. A major advantage with this is that the problem of where to draw the line between groups (disabled and non-disabled) is avoided. Furthermore, this type of measure will be able to capture the total activity limitation in the entire population and not only among those who qualify as being disabled. This will in turn have a great potential for mainstreaming disability research, as the phenomenon in question (activity limitation/restriction in social participation) will be measured and perceived as an issue for everyone. It is also suggested that the ICF based measures on activity limitations (or restrictions in social participation) overcomes problems related to measuring the 'severity' of disability, both because it is theoretically based and because it produces an index with far better statistical properties than most other attempts at grading disability. This in turn makes the 'new' type of measure more useful in testing and developing models on disability, thus possibly also boosting theoretical development in the field. The weakness of this alternative is primarily that it is more complex to administer and not yet fully developed for a broader application. It is clearly not a strategy for censuses that place strict limitations on space allocated for disability related questions, but would be useful in surveys and in particular in relation to theoretically-based research questions.

While the suggested alternative way of measuring and studying disability has many advantages, it is not suggested that this should replace the 'traditional' way of collecting disability statistics. We argue that there is a need for alternative and complementary ways of measuring and studying disability and that the two strategies have both strengths and weaknesses. The existence of two 'research strategies' in this field will most likely contribute to reduce the conceptual confusion and thus bring high quality disability statistics one step nearer.

The ICF has thus been instrumental in expanding and developing the basis for disability statistics. It is, however, also important to bear in mind that, although including psychological factors in the model, ICF does not 'deliver' in this respect. Psychological factors are not included other that in the theoretical model. While ICF may be seen as an attempt to combine a medical and a social model of disability (Shakespeare 2004), the inability to measure psychological barriers represents an important challenge for disability statistics in the years to come.

Application of research is crucial in general and in particular when the focus is on poor disabled people in low-income countries. It is argued that a strong involvement and even control by DPOs and inclusion of disabled people at all stages of the research process will contribute strongly to the quality of the research, sense of ownership among DPOs and to the application of findings at different levels. It is further argued that including disabled people at all levels in research increases the relevance, as important competence and life experience is brought into the research process. Having disabled people as interviewers contributes to creating a climate conducive for information gathering that may positively influence the quality of the data, and they also provide affirmative role models to those disabled people interviewed.

Conclusions

Current disability statistics are far from robust or comparable globally and are particularly weak in low-income countries. There is a strong need for design, development, and standardisation of measures to be applied in both censuses and representative surveys. Important work in this regard is underway through the work by the Washington City Group and the DPO-initiated research in Southern Africa. It has been argued that it is important to go beyond the issue of prevalence and produce statistics that can compare and analyse differences in standards of living between people who are disabled and those who are non-disabled. The disability – living conditions – poverty link should be the number one priority for broadening disability statistics from the current focus which is largely on prevalence.

Measuring and screening for disability has been a long-standing issue within disability statistics. In light of the recent conceptual development it is suggested that further development of this field comprises both the 'traditional' dichotomisation between disabled and non-disabled people and a new approach where activity limitations and restrictions in social participation are treated as common phenomena. From the data analysis perspective, the research challenge lies in understanding disability as a multidimensional phenomenon that can be approached both as a dichotomous measure (disabled, not disabled) and as a continuous measure of activity limitations/participation restriction. In addition, these measures must be interpreted as relevant to the environment, society and culture from which they are derived.

Application of research takes place at different levels. The potential for influencing policy, implementation of policy and services in different areas is boosted by availability of high quality data. In general DPOs need to take the responsibility for application of research they themselves have initiated and commissioned. A grass-root research strategy is important in order to ensure relevance and anchor research among DPOs, their members and the public in general. The ability to apply research will, however, also be strongly influenced by the relationship between DPOs and researchers. The organisations rely on research competence to utilise disability statistics. It is thus important to establish a good working relationship between the two parties. This requires capacity building and a deliberate and mutually-agreed strategy on both sides.

Recommendations

Sufficient resources and international collaboration and co-ordination are two central prerequisites for development of relevant and applicable disability research in low-income countries. Grounding research through disabled people and their organisations and applying principles of participatory research are also of great importance for both credibility, relevance and applicability of research. Such a grass-roots strategy for disability research in low-income countries underpinned the Disability and Statistics Workshop in Gaborone in June 2005.

It is necessary to develop designs for disability statistics globally. This includes standardised measures on disability, as well as application of the ICF in disability research. Adaptation of research designs to fit the situation in low-income countries should be given priority.

Disability research in low-income countries should as far as possible be initiated and controlled by DPOs in the respective countries and/or regions. Principles derived from participatory research should be followed.

It is necessary to establish and develop collaboration between DPOs, researchers, national and regional authorities and international organisations in order to develop disability research as a discipline in low-income countries.

Application of disability research in low-income countries should be planned for and resources allocated for this purpose from the onset of the project. Methods and strategies for applying research in low-income countries should be further developed.

Focal points for disability research should be identified both among DPOs and the relevant research institutions.

Long-term commitment to capacity building among DPOs and researchers to establish and develop a strategic working relationship between the two is needed from international donors and researchers. Structures for developing this relationship should be developed.

DPOs will in particular need long-term training and capacity building in order to play a leading role in disability research. Researchers and research institutions involved in disability research need to be sensitised to the particular challenges inherent in participatory research.

References

For full bibliography
http://www.disabilitykar.net/research/thematic_stats.html

Coleridge, P., 1993. *Disability, Liberation, and Development.* Oxford: Oxfam.

DFID., 2000. *Disability, poverty, and development.* London/East Kilbride: DFID.

Durkin, M. S., Davidson, L. L., Hasan, Z. M., et. al., 1994. Validity of the Ten Questions screen for childhood disability: results from population-based studies in Bangladesh, Jamaica and Pakistan. *Epidemiology*, 5.

Eide, A. H., and Loeb M., 2005a. Data and statistics on disability in developing countries. SINTEF Report No. STF78 A054506. Oslo: SINTEF Health Research.

Eide, A. H., and Loeb M., 2005b. *Data and statistics on disability in developing countries*. Disability KaR. Available at: http://www.disabilitykar.net/research/thematic_stats.html

Eide, A.H., van Rooy, G., Loeb, M., 2003a. Living Conditions among people with disabilities in Namibia. A National, Representative Study. STF78 A034503, Oslo: SINTEF Unimed.

Eide, A.H., Nhiwaitiwa, S., Muderedzi, J., Loeb, M., 2003b. Living Conditions among people with activity limitations in Zimbabwe. A representative, regional study. STF78 A034512, Oslo: SINTEF Unimed.

Elwan, A., 1999. Poverty and Disability. A Survey of the Literature. Social Protection Discussion Paper Series No. 9932. Washington D C: the World Bank.

Erb, S., and Harris-White, B., 2001. The economic impact and developmental implications of disability and incapacity in adulthood. A village study from S. India. Paper to the workshop Welfare, demography and development, September 11–12, Downing College, Cambridge.

Helander, E., Mendis, P., Nelson, G., Goerdt, A., 1989. *Training in the community for people with disabilities*. Geneva: World Health Organisation.

Islam, S., Durkin, M. S., Zaman, S. S., 1993. Socioeconomic status and the prevalence of mental retardation in Bangladesh. *Mental Retardation*. 31, pp.412 – 417.

Loeb, M. and Eide, A., 2004. *Living Conditions among people with activity limitations in Malawi: A national representative study.* STF78 A044511. Oslo: SINTEF Health Research.

Metts, R. L., 2000. Disability issues, trends and recommendations for the World Bank. SP Discussion Paper No. 0007. Washington DC: World Bank.

NPC., 2000. Level of living conditions survey. Windhoek: Planning Commission.

Schneider, M., Claasens, M., Kimmie, Z., Morgan, R., Naicker, S., Roberts, A., McLaren, P., 1999. We also count! The extent of moderate and severe reported disability and the nature of disability experience in South Africa. Pretoria: Community Agency for Social Enquiry.

Shakespeare, T., 2004. Perspectives and challenges in disability research. Presentation at Research symposium on disabilities in a framework of development, poverty and human rights. Oslo, 7th and 8th December.

SIDA., 1995. Poverty and Disability. A position paper. Stockholm: Swedish International Development Authority.

SSA., 2001. Prevalence of disability in South Africa. Pretoria: Statistics South Africa.

Statistics Canada., 2002. A New Approach to Disability Data. Catalogue no. 89-578-XIE. Ottawa: Statistics Canada.

United Nations., 1994. The Standard Rules on the Equalization of Opportunities for Persons with Disabilities. New York: United Nations.

United Nations., 1982. World Programme of Action Concerning Disabled Persons. A/RES/37/52. New York: United Nations.

UNSD., 2003. The collection and dissemination of statistics on disability at the

United Nations Statistics Division: Proposal for the future. New York: United Nations Statistics Division.

UNSO., 1990. Disability statistics compendium on special populations groups. DISTAT.. Series Y, No. 4. New York: United Nations.

WHO., 1980. International Classification of Impairments, Disabilities, and Handicaps: A manual of classification relating to the consequences of disease. Geneva: World Health Organisation.

WHO., 2001. International Classification of Functioning, Disability and Health. Geneva: World Health Organisation.

World Bank., 1993. *World Development Report*. Washington DC: World Bank.

Yeo, R., Moore, K., 2003. Including Disabled People in Poverty Reduction Work: 'Nothing About Us, Without Us'. *World Development*, 31 (3).

Yeo, R., 2001. Chronic poverty and disability. Chronic Poverty Research Centre. Working Paper 4. Manchester: Institute of Development Policy & Program Coordination/CPRC.

CHAPTER 8

Promoting inclusion? Disabled people, legislation and public policy

Tomson Dube, Rachel Hurst, Richard Light and Joshua Malinga.

Since the late 1960s the politicised movement of disabled people has demanded social justice and equal rights – both civil and human. They recognised that traditional myths, fears and stereotypes defined disabled people as the problem that needed to be changed or eliminated, whilst the Disability Rights Movement identified disability as the social response to people with impairments – what is now known as the social model of disability.

The movement, therefore, challenged these traditional and negative orthodoxies by placing disability on the political agenda and advocating for policies, programmes and legislation to support rights and non-discrimination. The movement recognised that without the protection of national civil rights legislation and the support of programmes to ensure disabled people's full and equal participation in society, disabled people would continue to be left out of any pursuit of human rights and attempts at social development.

This pursuit of social justice and rights has been in marked contrast to programmes and policies for development, both by agencies and governments, which have primarily seen disability as an issue of service provision, segregation and 'special' treatment. Furthermore, despite considerable evidence that disabled people are the poorest of the poor, the Millennium Development Goals (MDGs) have not addressed poverty with regard to disabled people. As the former president of the World Bank, James Wolfensohn, has said:

> Unless disabled people are brought into the development mainstream, it will be impossible to cut poverty in half by 2015 or to give every girl and boy the chance to achieve a primary education by the same date - goals agreed to by more than 180 world leaders at the UN Millennium Summit in September 2000.

However, despite these pronouncements, disability rights and disabled people are not mentioned at all, either in the MDGs themselves or in most governmental action plans and policies with regard to development. Even where they are, there is little evidence that they have been implemented. (see Chapter 4)

Added to this invisibility of disability in mainstream development programmes and initiatives, has been the absence of the voice of disabled people. And yet it is the direct experience of disabled people that is essential in ensuring that policies and programmes affecting them are appropriate and inclusive (UN, 1983, 1992).

With respect to the last point, a review of national legislation is critical because, within the new aid instruments such as PRSPs, SWAps, etc., there is a strong emphasis on development strategies being formulated by governments working in partnership with civil society and donors. There are well-justified doubts about how this has worked in practice, especially in terms of their being genuine national ownership. Nonetheless, if DPOs, as part of civil society, are going to be able to get their agenda on the table, then having strong domestic civil rights legislation, as well as the kind of state support recommended in the UN Standard Rules (see below), is essential. Unless disabled people are in a position to lobby their governments effectively and by doing so ensure that those governments in turn indicate to donors that disability is a key concern that needs to be mainstreamed in all the various aid instruments, disability will continue to be ignored in development cooperation.

The problems outlined above and the continuing hostile and discriminatory environment made it our principal concern to consider why disabled people were being left off the mainstream development agenda and to recommend ways that this can be challenged. To do this we:

- set up a collaborative research process between representative organisations of disabled people to promote critical analysis of law, policy and its implementation (intended to have an impact beyond the limits of this project);
- undertook a systematic appraisal of the content and impact of disability legislation/policy on the lives of disabled people;
- investigated the nature and extent of disabled people's influence on the legislative and policy process;
- identified key strategies and techniques for exerting decisive influence on the legislative and policy process;
- elaborated the goals of policy makers and disabled people in the construction of legislation/policy, with particular emphasis on apparent synergy and/or dissonance between such goals; and

- provided 'best practise' examples.

Background

Ever since the United Nations produced the World Programme of Action in 1983, there has been much rhetoric in support of rights and justice for disabled people, although the evaluation of the UN Decade of Disabled People (1983-1992) showed that little of substance had actually been achieved (CSDHA 1992).

In the World Programme of Action, the UN estimated that 10% of the world's population were disabled people, although it was acknowledged that statistical evidence was difficult to analyse as there were differing definitions of who was a disabled person. Many countries, particularly in the developing world, did not have any statistics at all with regard to disabled people. Even today, very little health or social statistics data is disaggregated in relation to disability. (see Chapter 7)

The UN Standard Rules on Equalisation of Opportunities for Disabled Persons were formulated as guidance to member states on how they could implement the recommendations of the World Programme of Action. Of particular interest to our concerns is Rule 18, which specifically says that 'States should recognize the right of the organizations of persons with disabilities to represent persons with disabilities at national, regional and local levels. States should also recognize the advisory role of organizations of persons with disabilities in decision-making on disability matters.' The Rule then goes on to recommend at length how this should be done through encouraging and economically supporting disabled people's own organizations in their role as advocates and to ensure their inclusion in policy-making and social development, to promote their equality of opportunity.

Of crucial importance to disability rights and to the disabled individual are the UN human rights instruments which were introduced in 1948 to ensure that the horrors of the holocaust did not happen again and to set an ethical agenda whereby member states recognized and protected the right of every individual to life, freedom and dignity. However, although disabled people were one of the main targets of the eugenic movement, resulting in many being sterilised in the US and Europe, as well as being the first group to face the Nazi gas chambers, except in the Convention on the Rights of the Child, disabled people are not specifically mentioned as a discrete group requiring protection from discrimination. They are implicitly included in the 'and others' catch-all phrase at the end of non-discrimination articles of the various human rights instruments. But this has been completely ineffective. Research has shown that, except for recent work of the Committee on the Rights of the Child, monitoring of countries' implementation of human rights has not covered the rights of disabled people (Degener & Quinn 2002).

When delegates met for the first meeting for an elaboration of a convention on the rights of disabled people in New York in 2002, following a special report from the UN Human Rights Commission (Degener & Quinn 2002), there was considerable reluctance to believe that there was any real need for a convention. Government delegations saw disability rights in terms of service provision and health and were not persuaded of the economic or human rights imperatives. However, as can be seen from reports of the proceedings, the participation of the disabled people's organisations, working together in the International Disability Caucus, with their evidence of violations and testimonies from disabled people all over the world, (DAA 2002a) both changed that perception and ensured that the elaboration process continued with the IDC as an active partner. Besides acknowledging that disabled people deserved specific protection, Disabled Peoples' International's slogan 'Nothing About Us Without US' became common currency throughout the proceedings.

The real story of the status of disabled people needs to be told. And it needs to be told with strong, incontrovertible evidence to back it up. That is why the research findings here, and in more detail in the full report, are so important. This particular piece of policy and legislation research has been particularly fortunate in being able to draw on a vast amount of archived material documenting the direct experience of disabled lives gathered by DAA since 1992 and work done by other disabled researchers.

Methodology

There were a number of different strands to the way this piece of work was carried out. The main thrust was a detailed questionnaire sent to eight selected disability activists in six countries in Africa and Asia. These written responses were then followed up by informal discussion that provided essential sensitivity to the 'sub-text' of responses. Whilst we carefully avoided elevating such insight to the status of empirical fact, it has informed our choice of secondary sources and, indeed, stressed the need to reinforce the data revealed by this small-scale study with such sources.

The evidence gathered was supplemented by reference to the DAA archives, including the Human Rights Violations Database, policy and legislation library, disabled people's own testimonies and letters collected over the years from our readers in 164 countries. Various pieces of research already carried out by DAA were included (Cutler 2001, Lansdown, 2002,3), as was policy and legislation research carried out in South America by the International Disability Rights Consortium. Also of value to the project was the lived experience of all members of the Project Team within the disability rights movement both in their own countries and internationally. In fact it would have been impossible, in the time available, to produce such well evidenced research without reference to these personal and professional experiences.

In addition to the foregoing elements, the project also offered the opportunity to consider the current work, mentioned above, of developing a convention to promote the human rights of disabled people. Included in our considerations was the daily reading of an e-group set up by members of the IDC to gain a consensus on the views of disabled people. In passing Resolution 56/168, on a 'Comprehensive and integral international convention to promote and protect the rights and dignity of persons with disabilities' in 2001, the UN General Assembly was implicitly acknowledging that disabled people's equal enjoyment of internationally agreed human rights and fundamental freedoms could not be taken for granted. As we have said before, human rights are the background or guiding star to sustainable development and, particularly in the case of disabled people who have been missing from the development agenda, it is important that this convention reflects that link.

Main findings

FEAR OF REPRISAL

It is sobering to note, in a study directed at disabled people's participation in the policy process, that the majority of respondents expressed concern about the risk of repercussions if they were seen to be critical of their government. Unsurprisingly, respondents expressed little desire to discuss the nature of such repercussions, not least whether such consequences would attach to them or to the organisations they represent. To a large extent, we consider this distinction to be of limited practical import. That respondents feared any punitive response to their candour is, we believe, a critical research outcome in itself.

What is, perhaps, more alarming still, is that reprisal for 'upsetting the apple cart' has been a common theme in the routine work of DAA: from 'disap-pearances' in Latin America, as recorded on the DAA violations database, to exposure to administrative processes linked to the receipt of welfare benefits. In all cases, the clear signal that advocacy risks punishment is communicated. Such oppression is consistent with the way in which government goes about the routine business of governance in some states. However, before dismiss-ing the problem as only a regional anomaly, we believe that it is important to acknowledge that pre-existing evidence shows similar vindictiveness in states that make much of their status as 'liberal' democracies. (DAA 2002b)

This generally precarious position of disabled peoples' organisations [DPOs] in the policy process has been highlighted by the fear, expressed by a number of the respondents, that candid answers to the project survey would result in recriminations. The general lack of financial support and therefore, of capacity of DPOs in both the North and South, combine with this fear to severely constrain the ability of disabled people to take part in and effect progressive change in civil society generally and the development process in particular.

INTERNATIONALLY

As we have demonstrated in our background to this project, the UN has put in place, or is now elaborating, various instruments to further the rights and freedoms of disabled people. However, disability is not properly mainstreamed into the rest of the UN's work, particularly that of development (UNDP con-cerns itself only with rehabilitation), nor do disability issues have the necessary priority for proper implementation and resourcing. It is interesting to note that HIV & AIDS is high on the UN and development agendas, but people with that condition are not seen as disabled people, nor the condition as a disability issue. In fact, the disability legislation in India does not cover those with medical conditions such as HIV & AIDS - or cancer or heart disease. It is these national anomalies that make it so important that there is clarity at the UN level to confirm with national governments that disabled people are people too and deserving of human rights and to be included in development assistance.

At a very basic level, access to UN buildings is often difficult, if not impos-sible and information is not readily, if at all, available in alternate media. The mismatch between the resources available for NGO participation, at whatever level, and that available to governments – all of whom maintain permanent mis-sions in New York – and to the various business and professional organisations increasingly active at the UN, amplify the barriers to equal participation in the international community.

Although difficult to quantify but, we believe, no less pertinent, the UN has tended to replicate national and regional governmental policy by diminishing the expertise and contribution of disabled people and our representative organisations, to that of 'users' or 'consumers', rather than autonomous agents with an equal contribution to make. Disabled people are only seen as recipients of development, We have not been given the dignity of co-production.

Despite the difficulties associated with collaborative working at the Ad Hoc Committee, DPOs have made a substantial contribution to the process. Although the heterogeneity of the disabled community is rarely acknowledged in public policy, to say nothing of the regional and cultural diversity of an international movement of disabled people, DPOs have shown that collaborative working does produce critical analysis of governmental proposals.

As a result of the work of DPOs at the UN, not only has the scope and content of the draft convention been substantially changed to reflect the views and aspirations of disabled people, the process has demonstrably increased disability awareness in states across the globe. It has also served to counter ignorance, prejudice and benign neglect amongst policy-makers and diplomats involved in the process, as well as promoting a thoroughgoing review of accessibility to buildings, information and programmes at the UN (although only in New York). Finally it has contributed to the process of 'mainstreaming' disability in public policy.

Perhaps the greatest achievement of the DPOs directly engaged in the work of the Ad Hoc Committee has been in sharing information, advice and opinion through wide-ranging discussion, much of it through a web-based discussion group. As even the most cursory review of that discussion group will confirm, the contribution of activists, advocates and lawyers across the world has served to highlight the impact of textual proposals on disabled people.

Although, perhaps inevitably, the internet-based discussion is most vigorous between meetings of the Ad Hoc Committee, the internet has also been used extensively to provide daily briefings on the work of the Committee and the concerns of the DPOs present. This has allowed progress to be monitored globally and as it happens.

Acknowledging that there are still barriers to address, progress at the UN indicates that the Internet can provide an inexpensive and generally effective means to promote the inclusion and participation of disabled people. In this regard, it would certainly appear helpful to explore means of promoting 'virtual international communities' and in the particular case of disabled people, such technology offers the potential of greater engagement with the international community than is physically possible with the individual's local community. The converse is equally relevant, however: denying disabled people access to communication technology exacerbates their exclusion from the mainstream.

NATIONALLY

Most countries have multiple statutory enactments that deal with different aspects of disability rights. Some are based on a holistic constitution, though these constitutions do not always name disabled people as a specific group – a reflection of the UN human rights instruments. How the legislation or policy is produced varies but does not seem to have any impact on outcomes: disabled people are still systematically being denied their rights in every country in the world. (Lindqvist 2002) The important improvement is that in those countries where their rights are properly protected, disabled people do have an opportunity, however great the economic and social barriers, to be seen as equal and participating citizens.

The *International Disability Rights Monitor Regional Report of the Americas* was of particular interest, as the majority of the researchers were local disabled leaders who were able to contribute their own perspective. Overall legal protections in the region are good, influenced in the main by the Organization of American States' (OAS) Inter-American Convention On The Elimination Of All Forms Of Discrimination Against Persons With Disabilities, (June 1999) which compelled the creation of at least some disability legislation through the ratification process. By protecting disabled people under international law, the convention is an important regional instrument for the protection of disability rights. Article III of the Convention affirms that:

> To achieve the objectives of this Convention, the states parties undertake: 1. To adopt the legislative, social, educational, labor-related, or any other measures needed to eliminate discrimination against persons with disabilities and to promote their full integration into society...

Of the thirty-four States that could have ratified the Convention, only fifteen had done so, according to our latest check as at 24 May, 2005.

In addition to international law, the national constitutions of half the countries in the region specifically identify disabled people as the subjects of rights. Fourteen countries have passed additional laws that deal solely with protections, and most others include disability issues within other types of legislation. Canada, Chile, Costa Rica, Dominican Republic, Ecuador, Panama, Uruguay and the United States all have anti-discrimination legislation.

However, the researchers often identified a reliance on charity rather than rights to achieve equality of opportunity – absolving government of the duty to act - and most of the legislation lacks enforcement procedures.

Some disabled people are stripped of the right to vote, as well as a host of other rights. Argentina, Bolivia, Peru, and Uruguay classify people who are deaf and cannot speak as legally incapable. People with intellectual impairments can have their rights taken away in Brazil, El Salvador, Guyana, Jamaica, and Peru. People with a sensory disability, such as blind people, may face such treatment in El Salvador, Guatemala, and Guyana. Finally, Canada reports that disabled people whose health represents a potential financial burden to the state may not be allowed to immigrate. Evidence from DAA's Violations data base suggests that this restriction is also applied in other countries, such as Australia, France, Denmark and the UK.

Overall it is clear that implementation of legislation is invariably inadequately funded and/or subject to ineffective monitoring and enforcement. It appears that the mechanisms that exist in the areas examined as part of this project place too much reliance on disabled people's good will and voluntary effort.

The countries that responded to our questionnaire were at very different stages of the struggle for disability rights and the responses reflected their expectations and belief in what amounted to good practice. South Africa's response, in particular, was surprisingly negative about what they had achieved – which is considerable (see below) – so not surprisingly they also showed that their expectations were much higher and they were more aware of what was possible.

All responses to our questionnaires identified a good or excellent relationship at ministerial level but that was infrequently maintained with civil servants and rarely occurred at local level. However, this good relationship was not reflected in how they answered the other questions – except for Kenya and South Africa. They did not feel that they had really been listened to or their views taken properly into account. They all had serious concerns as to the non-implementation of the legislation and Nepal and Bangladesh both identified party-political tensions within their governments as a barrier to the advancement of disabled people's rights.

One of the issues that came out of the Inter-Americas' report (IDRM 2005) is that when a single-impairment group took the leadership in consultation and influence, that impairment was the only one properly reflected in the ensuing policy/legislation. This was particularly notable in Ecuador where parents of people with learning difficulties had been running services since 1950 and Argentina and Paraguay, among others, where the organizations of the blind were strong.

It was clear from all our research that disabled people's status (economic, social and political) is low. Even when supported by evidence of violations, their arguments are not given the credibility they deserve, as it is disabled people who are the real experts on the abuse of their rights. Several countries in South America reported that parents and charitable or rehabilitation organisations led by non-disabled people were more likely to be listened to than disabled people, something that would, we are sure, resonate with DPOs in other regions. It is only when they hold the same politically powerful positions as non-disabled people that their expertise is fully recognised and considered, as they are in South Africa and Uganda. South Africa has an Office on the Status of Disabled Persons under the direct control of the President and entirely staffed by disabled people. There are similar offices at the regional and local levels. Uganda has a Minister and five members of parliament and every regional and local governing body has at least two political officials who are disabled people.

Although DPOs report at least some involvement in drafting legislation and influencing policy over the past five years, such involvement has not been given similar status to that provided by 'professional' agencies and is extremely weak at the local level. Governments appear rarely to acknowledge a need to resource DPO inclusion in the consultative process or to recognise fully their expertise, often preferring to listen to the voice of single impairment organisations, particularly those of parents and non-disabled professionals with whom they can identify and relate easily rather than bother about access and attitudinal barriers when consulting with disabled people.

Information is not being communicated – in either direction – from the national governmental and DPO leadership level to grass-roots organisations. And several countries identified general political and economic factors for the low priority given by their governments to disability rights.

Some examples of good practice were found, particularly in South Africa and Uganda, where disabled people play a significant role in the institutions of government and at all levels, as we have described above. However, even in these countries respondents felt that 'the grass must be greener on the other side', that is, in 'developed' countries. This only demonstrates the lack of shared information worldwide on the realities of disabled lives. For example, disabled people in the North, though having better access to health care, services and benefits than their brothers and sisters in the South, are still overrepresented among the poor, denied access to proper education and many continued to be institutionalised and excluded.

Evidence

Non-discrimination legislation and a human rights perspective on disability underpin the disability rights movement's articulation of the social model of disability and the need for social change. However, social change will not happen without evidence of the realities, agreement on the concepts and monitoring of progress.

Some of the South American states (Bolivia, Costa Rica, El Salvador, Guyana,) had offices that were collecting evidence on violations of civil and human rights against disabled individuals. This data was used as a campaigning tool for ensuring effective legislation and services. Additionally, data from the DAA Human Rights Database added impetus to the initial stages of the elaboration of a convention on the rights of disabled persons.

Legislation – good practice

How the legislation is written has, inevitably, a pertinent bearing on its effectiveness. The concept of reasonable accommodation or adjustment (UK, USA, Canada, Australia) is increasingly being used as the most effective means of promoting accessibility – in its widest sense – and is supported by disabled people as being essential if there is to be real social change, as evidenced by the importance attached to this concept in debate at the UN Ad Hoc Committee.

Legislation that creates enforceable obligations, backed up by vigorous and accessible implementation and where necessary, reinforced by penalties sufficient to promote compliance, is crucial. Even where these are in place, many disabled people do not know of their rights or how to access them. As Canada and the UK have found, commissions dealing with enforcement of non-discrimination have inadequate resources to administer all complaints and have o prioritise their work. Nevertheless, these essential ingredients of enforcement did make a substantial difference to the efficacy of the legislation.

A social-model definition of disability, as appears in the legislation of South Africa, the Philippines and Zimbabwe, has addressed the problem of defining the protected class less restrictively. Many other countries, (notably India, as we have previously mentioned) leave some disabled people without protection or remedy. The Inter-American Convention definition also has a social-model component:

> The term 'disability' means a physical, mental or sensory impairment, whether permanent or temporary, that limits the capacity to perform one or more essential activities of daily life and which can be caused or aggravated by the economic and social environment.

This last definition emphasises the need for social change in place of charitable attitudes or compensatory policies.

Conclusion

Several recommendations emerge from the research which, if adopted, would ensure better rights and justice for disabled people:

In order to recognise the inherent humanity of disabled people and their rights and protections, all legislation should operate in a human rights dimension, ensuring non-discrimination, personhood and equality of opportunity.

The practical and fiscal benefits that flow from disabled people's inclusion in the consultation and influence agenda, at local, regional, and national levels can only be achieved with formal and appropriately resourced partnerships between governmental and DPO actors, especially at the local level – as recommended by Rule 18 of the UN Standard Rules.

A significant factor in the continued low status associated with disablement is the tendency to demean or degrade disabled people's contribution to the policy agenda. As recent research has indicated (Ásgeirsdóttir, 2003: 3 and Stapleton et al. 2004), the modest impact achieved by governmental disability programmes demands new paradigms and recognition of disabled people's contribution to the policy and governance process. A secondary effect of this is likely to be greater participation and inclusion, precisely the aim – if not the outcome – of existing and preceding programmes. The present low 'glass ceiling' for disabled people must be raised and enabling structures put in place – structures such as those in South Africa and Uganda, where the status of the disabled individual in relation to governance is one of equality with others.

Despite increasing legal activity in national, regional and international fora, there is insufficient evidence concerning the reality of 'disabled lives'. If policy is to be better directed – and practical outcomes achieved – there is a pressing need to obtain more data and/or to disaggregate data from pre-existing data sets. However, the collection and manipulation of data must not be allowed to become an end in itself or, indeed, a tactic deployed to delay effective action.

Legislation must be mandatory, adequately funded and subject to enforcement mechanisms that are accessible to disabled people and capable of imposing penalties adequate to the task of combating illegal discrimination.

It is increasingly clear that the social model of disability (Light 2002) lies at the foundation of disabled people's political campaigns around the world, with the result that any legislation or policy that fails to adopt a social model perspective will fail to address the expectations of disabled people.

Finally, unless the systems outlined above are put in place and implemented it will be virtually impossible for DPOs to be seen as equal or even legitimate players in civil society. If this happens, disabled people's concerns are less likely to get onto the development agenda, as this is increasingly delivered within a new aid structure. The instruments which make up this structure, especially PRSPs, are supposed to be devised by donors and governments working in concert with civil society organisations (CSOs). But if the civil and human rights of disabled people are not respected officially and their organisations remain unsupported, their ability to take part in the development process will be severely limited. In this case 'Without Us' could be dropped from the slogan of international disability movement, for in development cooperation there is then, in any meaningful sense, likely to be simply 'Nothing About Us …'.

References

Ásgeirsdóttir, B., 2003. Opening Speech: Transforming Disability into Ability – Results and conclusions from the OECD's study of disability policies for the working-age population in 20 member countries', *Conference on 'Transforming Disability into Ability: Policies to promote work and income security for disabled people*, Vienna, 6-7 March 2003, OECD.

Centre for Social Development and Humanitarian Affairs, (1992) *Final Report of evaluation of UN Decade of Disabled Persons*, Vienna, United Nations.

Cutler, G., 2001., Comparative study of disability rights legislation in 11 countries, DAA, London.

DAA., 2002a. Global Rights Campaign Testimonies. London: DAA.

DAA., 2002b. A Real Horror Story. Report from Violations Database. London: DAA.

Degener , T. and Quinn, G., 2002. *A Survey of International, Comparative and Regional Disability Law Reform*. Report to the UNCHR, Geneva.

International Disability Rights Monitor (IDRM)., (2005), IDRM Report on the Americas, Available at: www.cirnetwork.org/idrm/reports/americas/

Lansdown, G., 2002. *Disabled Children in South Africa, Progress in implementing the Convention on the Rights of the Child*. London: DAA.

Lansdown, G., 2002. *Disabled Children in Romania, Progress in implementing the Convention on the Rights of the Child,*.

Lansdown, G., 2003. *Disabled Children in Nepal, Progress in implementing the Convention on the Rights of the Child*. London, DAA.

Lansdown, G., 2003. *Disabled Children in El Salvador, Progress in implementing the Convention on the Rights of the Child*, London: DAA.

Light, R., 2002. Social Model or Unsociable Muddle. DAA. Available at: www.daa.org.uk

Lindqvist, B., 2002. Special Rapporteur's 3rd Monitoring Report, to UN Commission on Social Development. E/CN/2002/4. New York: UN.

Stapleton, D. C., Burkhauser R. V., & Houtenville A. J., 2004. Has the Employment Rate of People with Disabilities Declined?, Policy Brief, Employment and Disability. Washington DC: Rehabilitation Research and

Training Center for Economic Research on Employment Policy for Persons with Disabilities.

United Nations., 1983. World Programme of Action Concerning Disabled People. New York: UN.

United Nations., 1992. UN Standard Rules on Equalisation of Opportunities for People with Disabilities. New York: UN.

CHAPTER 9

The role and effectiveness of disability legislation in South Africa

Andrew K. Dube

The Disability Knowledge and Research Programme (Disability KaR) had a strong focus on mainstreaming of disability in development cooperation. This is one reason why considering the South African experience is so instructive, highlighting as it does the possibilities and challenges of mainstreaming disability in a country with one of the strongest disability movements in the world, disability-inclusive legislation and a variety of policies protecting and promoting the rights of disabled people. In addition, disabled people are involved at the highest levels of government. Although officially classed as a middle-income country and, therefore, not representative of other sub-Saharan countries or developing countries generally, South Africa does exhibit many of the problems associated with these countries, including high levels of both unemployment and poverty, as well as substantial income inequality (Hunter, May and Padayachee 2003).

The aim of this study was to consider the extent to which, given the aforementioned apparently favourable factors, legislation and policies have been implemented. If they have, has this resulted in real changes to the lives of disabled people? For example, looking at the work of both national and provincial governments over the period 1994 to 2004, have disabled people gained greater access to education, employment, transport and so on?

Besides complimenting other Disability KaR research, it is hoped the more detailed report upon which this chapter is based will provide the disability rights movement and government departments in South Africa with evidence, insights, knowledge and recommendations on what is needed to increase the effectiveness of the policies and legislation designed to improve the lives of disabled people.

Historical background

When the ANC came to power in 1994, as the first democratically elected government, one of the first things it did was to establish a Constitutional Assembly to discuss and debate the cornerstones of democracy in South Africa. The culmination of the Constitutional Assembly's work was the adoption of a new Constitution on 8 May 1996, which included in the Bill of Rights, under the subsection on equality, provisions that say neither the state nor any person can unfairly discriminate against various categories of people, including disabled people and that, 'National legislation must be enacted to prevent or prohibit unfair discrimination.' (Republic of South Africa 1996)

In this way there was official acknowledgement that disabled people have in the past, and may continue to be, discriminated against. The inclusion of disability in the Constitution led to disability becoming an important consideration in new legislation and in policy documents that make up South Africa's legal and policy framework. This in turn has had the potential to have a major impact, either directly or indirectly, on the lives of disabled people and has created opportunities to address inequalities.

The new constitutional framework also marked an important milestone in the struggle of disabled people to overcome their previous exclusion from mainstream society. As a 'historical moment' in the history of the disability rights movement in South Africa, the Constitution's recognition of disability reflects the struggle of disabled people to be treated equally. It has provided the basis from which new and often more complex struggles have been waged since 1994. These struggles have been directed towards overcoming the social and economic barriers that have resulted in widespread poverty and marginalisation of the majority of disabled people in South Africa. (Chalklen and Howell 2003)

The period since the 1994 elections has been a time of significant change in South Africa's history. There is probably not one sector of society where some level of transformation has not taken place. Changes have been implemented at the policy and legislative level as well as at the level of service delivery and government accountability.

It is not possible to discuss in detail the extensive array of activities that disability rights activists have been involved in during this period. The movement's strategic positioning in the political arena was achieved through a range of initiatives that included the following:

The establishment of the Office on the Status of People with Disabilities (OSDP),

The parliamentary presence,

The strengthening of a coordinated civil society interface with government and

Representation on key statutory bodies

All these initiatives opened up opportunities for disability issues to be raised and addressed in a number of key sectors.

While many gains have been made, each has required sustained commitment and ongoing struggles for the disability activists involved. Some of these struggles have been successful, while others remain areas that require continued pressure, input and monitoring by the disability sector.

Economic background

As mentioned above, despite being classed as a middle-income country, the experience of the majority of South African households is of outright poverty or of continuing vulnerability to being poor. (Camerer 1997) For example, in 2001 57% of the population lived below the poverty line. This was similar to the 1996 figure. (Human Sciences Research Council 2004) In addition, the poverty gap has increased over these years, the poor become poorer. This is consistent with the fact that the distribution of income and wealth in South Africa is among the most unequal in the world. The Gini coefficient (a measure of income distribution where 0 equals perfect equality and 1 perfect inequality) for all population groups has risen from 0.68 to 0.77 (1991-2001) (Human Sciences Research Council 2004). This situation is likely to affect not only the country's social and political stability, but also the development path it follows. Countries with less equal distributions of income and wealth tend not to grow as rapidly as those with more equitable distributions.

Under apartheid, South Africa was a deeply divided and unequal society. The inequalities and divisions arose from a political, economic and social system that aimed to keep black people subservient to white people and deny the former access to basic political rights as well as the opportunity to share in the country's wealth. This meant that lives of black and white disabled people under apartheid were very different, mirroring the enforced inequalities in the country (Chalklen and Howell 2003). Although South Africa has undergone a dramatic economic, social, and political transition in the last decade, many of the economic distortions introduced by apartheid continue to reproduce poverty and perpetuate inequality. As indicated above, both have in fact become worse.

However, it must also be recognised that under apartheid all disabled people, black and white, were discriminated against and marginalised because of their impairments. In particular, they had limited access to fundamental socio-economic rights such as employment, education and appropriate health and welfare services. This kind of discrimination and marginalisation occurred because disabled people in general were seen as people who were sick or in need of care, rather than as 'normal' citizens with equal rights and responsibilities (Chalklen and Howell 2003).

The research upon which this chapter is based investigated the extent to which the economic and social condition of disabled people in South Africa has been ameliorated through policies and legislation. In particular, the focus is on whether this has resulted in providing better access to employment and government services for disabled people, such as education and welfare benefits.

Methodology

Extensive desk research and a literature review were conducted in order to identify key information that relates to the delivery of services to disabled people through implementation of policies and legislation. This was complimented by research questionnaires and interviews with key respondents in government departments in four provinces (Gauteng, KwaZulu/Natal, Eastern Cape, and Western Cape) in order to determine the extent to which these departments have implemented disability strategies. These provinces were chosen due to the need to achieve a balance between urban (represented by Western Cape and Gauteng) and rural areas (KwaZulu/Natal and Eastern Cape Provinces). They also exhibit strikingly different poverty levels, the former provinces with respectively 32% and 42% of the population below the poverty line and the latter rural provinces with figures of 61% and 72%. (Human Sciences Research Council 2004) The more detailed findings from this particular aspect of the research can be found in the full report.

Extent of disability in South Africa

As is common in almost all developing countries, statistical data on the prevalence of disability in South Africa is neither comprehensive nor accurate. Estimates of the number of disabled people in South Africa vary from 5.9% (CASE 1997) to 12%. The 2001 census found that the total number of disabled people had decreased slightly between 1996 and 2001, from 2,657,714 to 2,255,973. This decrease might reflect the sampling methods used, or the fact that there is widespread confusion on the definition of disability, or other factors.

Although differences in definitions of disability and problems of data collection make national comparisons unreliable, the percentage of disabled people in South Africa appears to be far higher than in other Southern African countries. For example, the prevalence of disability in Zambia is 1.6% and in Malawi 2.9%. (Eide, van Roy and Lobe 2003, p. 29). It is impossible to account for this marked difference. It could be due to statistical anomalies and/or the fact of South Africa's relative economic prosperity, as internationally there seems to be a distinct positive correlation between the latter and the proportion of disabled people. (Albert 2004, p.3 f/n)

The White Paper on an Integrated National Disability Strategy
In November 1997, the government adopted the White Paper on an Integrated National Disability Strategy (INDS). It represents a paradigm shift in the conceptualisation of disability from the medical or welfare model of disability to a social model approach.

The foreword, by the then Deputy President Thabo Mbeki, is eloquent in setting out the government's thinking on disability. He wrote:

The concept of a caring society is strengthened and deepened when we recognise that disabled people enjoy the same rights as we do and that we have a responsibility towards the promotion of their quality of life.
We must stop seeing disabled people as objects of pity but as capable individuals who are contributing immensely to the development of society.
Throughout the world disabled people are organising themselves to engage society on the question of their fundamental rights. ...The emphasis is on a fundamental shift in how we view disabled people, away from the individual medical perspective, to the human rights and development of disabled people.
As a government we endorse these principles. (Republic of South Africa 1997)

The INDS provided government and society as a whole with guidelines to promote non-discriminatory development planning, programme implementation and service delivery. Although it has not yet been set out in legislation, government departments are required to formulate their disability policies and strategies in line with the provisions of the INDS and the core business of the department concerned.

Apart from the INDS, the government has passed legislation and formulated policies to address the needs of disabled people. These are either specific to disabled people (particularly in the field of training, employment creation, education, and social security) or general mainstream laws that can be utilised by disabled people. The examples given below represent only a small proportion of such legislation and policy. They were selected because data on their implementation is available.

Social Assistance Act No. 59, 1992

The Social Assistance Act, 1992 provides for social assistance to individuals, national councils and welfare organisations. The Act was amended in 1994 and again in 1997. Disabled people are offered assistance under this legislation through various types of disability grants.

The total number of people receiving social grants of all kinds rocketed from 2.9 million in April 2000 to 7.9 million in April 2005. It is anticipated that this number will increase by more than 20% per annum (Republic of South Africa 2004a).

According to the National Treasury, since 2000/01, spending on disability grants has increased from R4.0 billion to an estimated R10.3 billion by 2003/04, an overall increase of more than R6.3 billion over the period. Between the years 2000 and 2003 the number receiving grants doubled from about 600,000 to 1.2 million. In all provinces, except Northern Cape where coverage was already exceptionally high at the beginning of the period, disability spending more than or nearly doubled between 2000/01 and 2003/04. Spending grew particularly rapidly in Free State and KwaZulu-Natal, two provinces with extremely high rates of poverty. There is real concern that this level of spending is not sustainable in the long term (Republic of South Africa 2004a).

The Social Assistance Act is probably one of the most talked about pieces of legislation in South Africa. The Act is administered by the Department of Social Development's social assistance programme and it provides the legislative framework for awarding the *disability grant, care dependency grant, and grant-in-aid*. The disability grant is for adults from the age of 18 years who are unlikely to find employment because of their impairment and have no or limited sources of income. The care dependency grant is for families or carers of disabled children and the grant-in-aid is for disabled adults who might or might not be receiving a disability grant. In addition, the Department of Social Development gives a grant for social relief distress.

The amount of money spent and the numbers covered by the disability grants has increased, suggesting that at least for disabled people, this legislation has been successfully implemented. Nonetheless, a great deal of criticism has been levelled at how the grant system operates.

Looking at the Care Dependency Grant (CDH), Teresa Guthrie of the Child Health Policy Institute has argued that the eligibility criteria has been drawn so narrowly that most disabled children are excluded from this grant, including those with HIV/AIDS.(Dube 2005) Furthermore, although the Integrated National Disability Strategy calls for a social-model/human rights approach to disability, the CDH assumes a purely medical model focus, ignoring any social or economic considerations. (Child Health Policy Institute 2000) Because this benefit is means tested and those operating the system are poorly trained, this leads to inconsistency as well as degrading treatment. Such criticisms, as well as the problems caused by delays and lack of inter-sectoral collaboration, can be said to characterise all the disability grants.

The Employment Equity Act, 1998
The Employment Equity Act (EEA) has two principal purposes, namely:
    To implement positive measures to eliminate discrimination in employment;
    To provide guidelines for companies to promote occupational equity by encouraging the equitable representation of employees who are disabled as well as in terms of race and gender.

The EEA sets out to protect disabled people against unfair discrimination on the grounds of their impairment and entitles them to affirmative action measures. Employers may not discriminate unfairly against employees or applicants for employment because the employer suspects or believes, whether the belief or suspicion is correct or not, that the applicant or employee has an impairment that amounts to a disability. Furthermore, they can't discriminate against people that have been disabled, or if they are, or have been, associated with other people who are, or have been, disabled

Employment equity centres on a ban on unfair discrimination of any kind in hiring, promotion, training, pay, benefits and retrenchment, in line with Constitutional requirements. In addition, employment equity entails introducing measures to encourage employers to undertake organisational transformation to remove unjustified barriers to employment for all South Africans, and to accelerate training and promotion for individuals from historically disadvantaged groups.

Achieving employment equity objectives means confronting a legacy of unequal education, job reservation, racism, and discrimination in the workplace. Because of this the EEA Act recommends that at least 2% of all employees in companies with more than 50 workers should be disabled (Republic of South Africa 1998). To help achieved this goal a final draft of the Code of Good Practice for the Employment of Persons with Disabilities, was published in 2002. Two year later this was supplemented with the Technical Assistance Guide to the employment of Persons with Disabilities was released. These codes aim to assist employers in the recruitment of disabled people.

It would seem that the current positive policy and legislative environment has created unprecedented employment opportunities for disabled people, as South African employers, for the first time, are encouraged to employ disabled people (du Toit 2005) Despite this positive policy environment, talented and qualified disabled people continue to face unemployment. In fact, the Department of Labour estimates that only *1 % of disabled people are employed* in the formal sector of the economy.

One of the many reasons for this appalling state of affairs is that equality in employment cannot succeed without a national education and training system that supports the development of every individual in society. A critical look at how employers and training providers have provided education, training and work experience in the past indicates that education and training provision for disabled persons has not always been responsive to the demands of the economy, nor has it always linked theory and practice (Republic of South Africa 2003).

The enormity of the task is demonstrated if we consider that according to the information from national departments and provincial administrations, disabled people comprise only 0.25% of their employees, well below the 2% that should be achieved by 2005. In respect of the 6 provincial administrations that were reviewed in detail for this study, employment of disabled people averages only 0.16% (South Africa Public Service Commission 2002).

According to the Commission for Employment Equity (CEE) in its report for 2002-2003, the proportion of disabled people in senior management positions was extremely low. They conclude that not enough skills development interventions are being implemented to accelerate the development of designated groups, for the purpose of promotion into senior and top management levels.

Qualitative data also suggests that inadequate attention is being paid to the transformation of the workplace. This should include strategies to eliminate unfair discrimination through training of management and all staff on attitude change and diversity management and generally introducing workplace changes that are aimed at affirming human diversity (Republic of South Africa 2003).

Employer reports and independent studies, such as the annual reports of the CEE, suggest that progress towards the achievement of the objectives of the Employment Equity Act has been minimal. The Commission was concerned that '… if we continue at this pace employment equity will become a challenge for decades' (Republic of South Africa 2003)

It is hoped that if the workplace environment embraced the transformation agenda by combining their compliance with the Skills Development Act, the Broad Based Black Economic Empowerment Act and diversity management strategies, the pace of achieving employment equity will be accelerated significantly.

Skills Development Act, 1998
The Skills Development Act, 1998 would seem to be precisely what is needed to address some of the problems identified in achieving greater equality in employment, as its central purpose is to improve the employment prospects of persons previously disadvantaged by unfair discrimination and to redress those disadvantages through training and education. In this regard, disabled people were to be targeted. According to the *National Skills Development Strategy Implementation Report* (Republic of South Africa 2003b), equity targets underpin every objective of the National Skills Development Strategy (NSDS). These targets state that the beneficiaries of the strategy should be 85% black, 54% female, and 4% people with disabilities. However, like the disability target under the EEA, this one too has yet to be achieved For example, in 2003/04, in total 87% of those who participated in NQF level one learning programmes during this period were black, 33% were female and only 0.1% were disabled (Republic of South Africa 2004b). The figure is even worse for those who completed structured training in 2002/3. Only 0.08% were disabled people.

A facilitated focus group discussion convened by this research project explored some of the reasons why government targets have largely remained unmet. The participants identified the following factors:

• disability unemployment is a result of low level skills among disabled

people;
• there is lack of initiative by the private and public sector;
• negative employer attitudes towards disabled persons;
• special and mainstreamed schools are in disarray, with learning standards dropping to unacceptable levels; and
• individual efforts by the disability sector are fragmented and ineffective.

An important issue is that the disability policies might not correlate what is happening in the real world. The disability movement first got disability into the Employment Equity Act and thereafter also ensured a disability component in the learnerships programmes. However, reality has shown that many disabled people might even not qualify for these learnerships, hence the need for a pre-learnership programme. Such a project is currently being developed and the plan is to present it directly to the Ministry of Labour.

It was noted in both data from the Public Service Commission and CEE reports that the general trend is that disabled people tend to be employed in the less skilled jobs, with very few disabled employees at management levels.

South African Schools Act, 1996
The South African Schools Act of 1996 provides for the inclusion of students with special educational needs. Public schools are required by law to admit all students and provide the necessary educational requirements without discrimination. At the level of implementation this law and associated policies have experienced many difficulties. The most apparent are the lack of resources, both financial as well as human, particularly in the form of trained educators. This has meant that disabled children are still not fully integrated into the public school system.

Low educational levels exacerbate unemployment among disabled people. In the CASE study report, the figures on school attendance indicate that primary school is the most accessible education level with 79% of respondents attending mainstream primary school and 12% special school and only 5% not attending school at this level. Pre-school and high school are generally not accessed as well, with 40% and 44% respectively of respondents attending mainstream schools at these levels. A similar number of disabled children attend special schools at pre-school and high school as at primary school (10% and 9% respectively) (CASE 1999).

This does not in any way mean that just because many disabled children attend primary school in the mainstream system, that inclusive education has been achieved or that disabled children have been catered for. As pointed out by the National Commission on Special Needs in Education and Training and the National Committee on Educational Support Services (NCSNET/NCESS), this inclusion is an ad hoc solution which does not deal with the issues of special educational need, nor impairment. There are just no other services and so disabled children are on the whole 'dumped' onto the mainstream schools whether by their parents or the education system (CASE 1999).

According to the CASE report, a comparison between the percentage distribution of disabled and non-disabled people by income and by level of education was made, which showed the impact impairment has on income. For instance, someone with a degree has only a 7% likelihood of being in the lower income category if they are not disabled. However, this increases to 22% if they are disabled. A disabled person with no education has a 60% likelihood of being in the lowest income category, versus 44% for a non-disabled person (Case 1999).

The report also details the range of difficulties facing disabled students at high school level. No or little provision exists for learners who are disabled and they are not provided with the necessary support. Besides making life extremely difficult for the student who has special educational needs, this situation places additional strain on teachers who are struggling to cope with large classes. A support system in high schools is imperative for disabled students to learn effectively.

White Paper 6 on Special Needs Education (2001)
Special needs education is a sector where the ravages of apartheid remain most evident. Here, the segregation of students on the basis of race was extended to incorporate segregation on the basis of impairment. Apartheid special schools were thus organised according to two segregating criteria – race and disability. In accordance with apartheid policy, schools that accommodated white disabled students were extremely well-resourced, whilst the few schools for black disabled students were systematically under-resourced.

The impact of this policy was that only 20% of disabled students were accommodated in special schools. The World Health Organisation has calculated that between 2.2 % and 2.6 % of learners in any school system could be identified as disabled. An application of these percentages to the South African school population would project an upper limit of about 400,000 disabled students.

Current statistics show that only about 64,200 disabled students are accommodated in about 380 special schools. This indicates that potentially 280,000 disabled students are unaccounted for (Republic of South Africa 2001).

The White Paper outlines what an inclusive education and training system is. It also provides the framework for establishing such an education and training system, details a funding strategy and lists the key steps to be taken in establishing an inclusive education and training system for South Africa.

The vision of an inclusive education and training system can only be developed over the long term and the actions to be taken in the short to medium term must provide models for later system-wide application. The short-term to medium-term actions will also provide further clarity on the capital, material and human resource development and consequently the funding requirements of building an inclusive education and training system.

The complexity of the process in terms of changing attitudes and behaviour, retraining educators, principals, administrators and teacher educators and also the effects on learners, parents and communities and not least the resource and capacity implications, all need to be researched, monitored and evaluated.

Despite the progressive suggestions contained in the White Paper, as of yet little has been done to implement them and disabled students continue to be badly served by the education system.

Conclusions

Support for the formulation and adoption of various disability policies in South Africa has been excellent. This positive policy environment should have created a greater awareness of the needs of disabled people as well as the unique opportunities for them across a wide range of issues. However, with the exception of a few policies such as the Social Assistance Act, the implementation of these policies has had a marginal impact on the lives of the majority of disabled people in South Africa. Of particular note is the fact that there are capacity constraints at programmatic level that limit the effective implementation of policy. Policy implementation issues are not addressed consistently for various reasons at different levels of government. These reasons include limited conceptual understanding, poor championing, inadequate or inappropriate institutional arrangements and a general lack of capacity. The result has been an exceptionally high degree of policy evaporation with respect to disability.

Other factors that have contributed to the poor implementation of legislation and policies, are that the definition and nature of disabled people's participation have not been adequately reviewed and articulated and the policy requirements for disability mainstreaming are not satisfactorily linked to performance management, thereby undermining commitment to implementation.

In addition, legislation and policies are not implemented, due to a lack of allocated fiscal resources and commitment. A pertinent example is the Policy on Inclusive Education – the White Paper was released in 2001 and yet implementation remains fragmented.

Where successful implementation has occurred, it has largely been due to political support by the ministers and senior civil servants in charge of departments and/or the sustained commitment and strong advocacy by the disability sector, led by Disabled People South Africa (DPSA).

Generally, the development of disability policies within government departments at both national and provincial levels is at a formative stage, with the majority of departments having no workable strategies for implementation. Because of this and the factors outlined above, most disability policy has tended to be stuck on the page, rather than being used to improve the lives of disabled people. As shown in Chapter 4, the South African experience is replicated in many developing countries, where the promises held out by find-sounding policies remain unfulfilled. This continues to remain a challenge for both the national and international disability movements and the people they represent.

References

Albert, B., The social model of disability, human rights and development. Disability KaR Briefing Note. Available at: http://www.disabilitykar.net/research/red_social.html

CASE., 1999. Disability survey for the Department of Health: 'We also count' The extent of moderate to severe reported disabilities and the nature of the disability experience in South Africa. Johannesburg. Executive Summary Available at :http://www.case.org.za/publications2.html

Camerer, L., 1997 Poverty and Social Security in South Africa. *Commercial Crime in South Africa*. Monograph No. 15, Institute for Security Studies. Available at: http://www.iss.org.za/index.php?link_id=23&slink_id=533&link_type=12&slink_type=12&tmpl_id=3

Chalklen, C. and Howell, S., 2003. Disability - our voices, our rights: The history of Disabled People South Africa and the struggles of the disability rights movement in South Africa (1980 – 2001). Unpublished mss. DPSA.

Child Health Policy Institute and Black Sash., 2000. Issue Paper on Social Security for Children in South Africa Prepared for the Commission of Enquiry for a Comprehensive Social Security System in South Africa. Available at: http://web.uct.ac.za/depts/ci/pubs/pdf/poverty/workpap/issue.pdf

du Toit, M., 2005. Disability Employment Equity. Unpublished mss..

Dube, Andrew K., The role and effectiveness of disability legislation in South Africa. Disability KaR. Available at: http://www.disabilitykar.net/research/small_sa.html

Eide, A.H., van Rooy, G., Loeb, M., 2003a. Living Conditions among people with disabilities in Namibia. A National, Representative Study. STF78 A034503, Oslo: SINTEF Unimed.

Human Sciences Research Council., 2004. Fact Sheet: Poverty in South Africa. Available at: http://www.sarpn.org.za/documents/d0000990/index.php

Hunter, N., May, J., and Padayachee, V., 2003. Lessons for PRSP from Poverty Reduction Strategies in South Africa. Report to the African Learning Group on Poverty Reduction Strategies, Economic Commission for Africa, Unpublished mss, School of Development Studies, University of KwaZulu-Natal. Available at: http://www.sarpn.org.za/documents/d0000672/index.php

Republic of South Africa, 1996. Constitution. Available at: http://www.polity.org.za/html/govdocs/constitution/saconst. html?rebookmark=1

Republic of South Africa, Office of the Deputy President., 1997. Integrated National Disability Strategy White Paper. Available at: http://www.info.gov.za/whitepapers/1997/disability.htm

Republic of South Africa, Department of Labour., 1998. The Employment

Equity Act. Available at:
http://www.labour.gov.za/act/index.jsp?legislationId=5954&actId=8191

Republic of South Africa, Department of Education., 2001. *Education White Paper6. Special Needs Education. Building an Inclusive Education and Training System.* Available at:
http://www.info.gov.za/whitepapers/2001/educ6.pdf

Republic of South Africa, Department of Labour., 2003. *Commission for Employment Equity Report 2002-2003.* Available at:
http://www.labour.gov.za/reports/report.jsp?report_id=8524&parCat_id=8522

Republic of South Africa, Department of Labour., 2003b. Commission of Social Security., *National Skills Development Strategy Implementation Report, April 2002 – March 2003.* Available at:
http://www.psc.gov.za/docs/reports/2004/disability_equity/exec_summary.pdf.

Republic of South Africa, Department of Labour., 2004b. Commission of Social Security., *National Skills Development Strategy Implementation Report, April 2003 – March 2004.* Available at:
http://www.info.gov.za/otherdocs/2004/nsdsreport.pdf.

Republic of South Africa, National Treasury., 2004b. Trends in intergovernmental finances address to the national council of provinces, speech by Trevor Manuel, Minister Of Finance, September. Available at:
http://www.treasury.gov.za/speech/2004090101.pdf

South Africa Public Service Commission., 2002. *Report on Disability Equity in the South African Public Service.* Available at:
http://www.psc.gov.za/docs/reports/2004/disability_equity/exec_summary.pdf.

CHAPTER 10

Participation of disabled people in the PRSP/PEAP process in Uganda

Andrew K. Dube

The research on which this chapter is based documents the experience of the Ugandan disability movement's engagement with the development of the country's most recent (2005) Poverty Reduction Strategy Paper (PRSP). The work was undertaken in response to the interest in the Ugandan experience expressed by disabled people's organisations (Dpos) at the Disability KaR's Malawi Roundtable (Disability KaR 2004).

PRSPs, first introduced in 1999 by the World Bank and the International Monetary Fund (IMF), are aid documents that set out low-income countries' plans to tackle poverty. They are a central element in being able to draw down budget support from international donors. PRSPs are supposed to be formulated through consultation between civil society organisations (CSOs), national governments and international donors, particularly the World Bank and the IMF. Uganda's experience is of particular interest because its version of PRSP, the Poverty Eradication Action Plan (PEAP), predated the official launch of the new document by two years and, in many respects, provided the model for the new approach. Partly because of this, Uganda has become 'the jewel in the crown' of the post-structural-adjustment aid regime. (Nyamugasira and Rowden 2002).

With respect to disability, Uganda is also of special interest. It has perhaps the most politically integrated disability sector in the world. The National Union of Disabled Persons of Uganda (NUDIPU) is an extremely high-profile national umbrella organisation and the rights of disabled people are enshrined in the Constitution. Furthermore, disabled people serve as elected representatives at all levels of government, from the village to the national parliament. In 1998 there were more than 45,000 disabled people involved. (Lwanga-Ntale 2003).

Interestingly, considering the above, the disability movement had not been involved in the formulation of the PEAP, either initially (1997) or during it its revision in 2000. It was only when the third PEAP was being developed that DPOs were invited to participate.

DPOs felt that participating in the PRSP process was very important in shaping future government policy interventions and, therefore, they wanted to take advantage of the opportunity. As a group with key concerns and as partners in the development process of the country, they needed to ensure that the government heard these concerns and took them into consideration.

Political and Economic Context

There have been a great many criticisms of the PRSP process, the primary one being that it is simply neo-liberal structural readjustment repackaged. (Ambrose 2000). It is not our intention here to enter into this debate. However, while the weaknesses in the consultation aspect of the PEAP will be discussed below, it must be pointed out that in the case of Uganda the development and implementation of the PEAP has coincided with impressive economic growth and a marked fall in poverty.

In the fifteen years from 1986/7 gross domestic product grew at an annual rate of 6.8%, at the same time as there was a structural shift from agriculture to small business, industry and other sectors. Between 1992/93 and 2002/03 the income poverty index fell from 56% to 34%, although it showed a slight increase to 38% in the last three years of that period. Over these latter years, as the rate of economic growth slowed, income inequality grew, with the Gini coefficient (a measure of income equality, with 1 being perfect inequality and 0 perfect equality) rising from .40 to .43 (Okida, Seewanyana, etc. al 2004).

Besides starting from such an extremely low socio-economic position after decades of civil war and political instability, the key element in explaining the relative success of pro-poor growth in Uganda is to be found in the political situation there. As set out in detail by Piron and Norton (Piron and Norton 2004, p.19),

> In order to understand the political conditions under which the PEAP is operating, we have to bear in mind Uganda's violent past and the fundamental importance of nation-building by the current Movement regime. This past has been used to legitimise a consensus-based, no-party political system, where security and poverty reduction are seen as essential for national unity. Concentration of political power in the Executive, combined with the President's commitment to poverty reduction, has created a favourable political environment.

There is, therefore, a clear political interest being served by adhering to poverty reduction and the PRSP process. International donors too have a political agenda which is advanced by what has happened in Uganda. 'Uganda has become one of the role models of structural adjustment and neo-structural- adjustment policies in the form of PRSPs and budget support. The perceived success of its poverty eradication policies has become closely intertwined with current international development assistance trends.' (Piron and Norton 2004, 16)

Methodology
The research was conducted within an emancipatory research framework. That meant engaging disabled people and DPOs from the onset and all the way through the process. As mentioned above, the initial idea for the project came from DPOs and other stakeholders who met in Malawi and were interested in what lessons could be learned from the PRSP experience in Uganda, lessons which would be of practical value in their own countries.

The consultative process involved working sessions with individual disabled people's organisations in Uganda, completion of a key informant interview questionnaire and discussions with MPs and the Ministry of Disability and the Elderly, as well as donor agencies that supported NUDIPU in the PRSP exercise. NUDIPU also established of a project reference group to gather additional information and feedback on the research process and content. Additional data was gleaned through the more traditional methods of a literature review and collection of official documents.

The main constraint on the research was one of time. We had only three months to formulate, organize and carry out the work. While we feel the results are sound, there is still a great deal of work that needs to be done on this topic.

Participation of disabled people in the PRSP/ PEAP process
In 1987 the National Union of Disabled Persons of Uganda – NUDIPU – was formed by 17 groups of disabled people as an umbrella organisation to provide a united voice for the disability movement. It was established as a cross-impairment body, as it was felt that while disabled people might have different specific needs related to their impairments, they all shared the common experience of discrimination and the only way to deal with this was together. Before this time disabled people were not seen as active players in their own affairs, but primarily as objects of charity. NUDIPU was to challenge this understanding (Nayiga Florence-Ssekabira 2000).

The expressed aim of the organisation is to fight negative attitudes, discrimination, to improve the welfare of disabled people and to advocate for equalisation of opportunities, involvement and participation in policy planning and implementation of disability programmes in close cooperation with government, NGOs, and the general public.

Partly because of NUDIPU's strong advocacy and its raising the issue of disability and human rights, this question was taken up in Article 35 of the Uganda Constitution 1995 which states that 'Persons with disabilities have a right to respect and human dignity and the State and society shall take appropriate measures to ensure that they realise their full mental and physical potential.'

Disability issues in Uganda are now part and parcel of the country's general concerns and have to be addressed, at least on paper, in national and local policies and programmes. A whole raft of legislation now includes provisions specifically addressing the needs and rights of disabled people. Each of these aims to mainstream disability and provides regulations aimed at improving accessibility of services to disabled people.

As mentioned above, given the relatively favourable position achieved by the disability movement, it is curious that it was not until the most recent PEAP process that a co-ordinated effort was made to get disabled people included in mainstream poverty eradication programmes. However, once it was decided by NUDIPU that this should be a priority, respondents told us that their leaders lobbied strenuously and were finally successful in getting a seat at the table.

As part of this lobbying process, it was pointed out to the authorities that DPOs possessed certain unique capacities, such as first-hand knowledge, a high level of awareness and privileged information, together with intellectual and analytical skills. These were complemented by particular qualities, including commitment, creativity, inventiveness, and willingness to share information.

NUDIPU strategy was not only to get a seat at the table, but also to make sure their participation was built around the following elements:

• close interaction with the centre of government;
• active mobilisation of district and sub-counties; and
• Setting up disability indicators for the PEAP, particularly, but not limited to, universal primary education (UPE), HIV and AIDS and agriculture.

There was also a realisation of the need for accountability, meaning that DPOs had an obligation to ensure that the process of drawing up the PRSP explicitly reflected the needs and priorities of disabled people, along with the needs of other vulnerable groups. In addition, accountability would help ensure that realistic mechanisms were put in place to hold government and service providers answerable for the delivery of policies and goods and for the spending of public funds. This process also ensured that DPOs were prepared for involvement in monitoring how PRSP strategies are implemented and whether anti-poverty commitments are being fulfilled for the benefit of disabled people.

DPO participation in the formal PEAP process was in the context of a government initiated Civil Society Task Force, composed of international and national NGOs operating in Uganda, with the Uganda Debt Network becoming the lead agency for civil society participation. The Task Force also formed part of the Steering Committee that drove the whole process. Specific activities included:

- running consultations with grassroots groups as a complementary initiative to a series of workshops with local government officials run by the Government;
- a media campaign to disseminate information on the PRSP process and collect views from a wide cross section of society; and
- consultations with special interest groups, such as DPOs and those involved in conflict resolution and environmental issues, and other CSOs, such as the National Union of Trade Unions.

The consultations indicated that DPOs and other civil society stakeholders viewed employment creation as a priority concern along with mechanisms for civil society participation in monitoring of the programme. The results were presented to the Technical (drafting) Committee, which incorporated them into the PEAP/PRSP, notably including a whole section on participation and monitoring written by civil society. Further civil society initiatives took place outside the activities of the Task Force and drew in contributions from over 200 other NGOs and community-based organisations.

Senior NUDIPU staff played a useful role in the PEAP process. The staff handled technical work in terms of pulling together the views of the various disabled people's organisations who participated. NUDIPU personnel also attended and provided inputs into the stakeholder and sectoral meetings and

consultations on the PEAP process.
In addition, NUDIPU staff:

* provided feedback to leadership on the PEAP process;
* worked with employees of other organisations in the disability movement;
* followed up with government departments on inputs from the disability movement to ensure that disability components were captured;
* shared and disseminated information on the PRSP/ PEAP processes; and
* garnered support from other PEAP stakeholders to impress upon the NGO Forum the need to include disability components in consultative group presentations.

The level of involvement of disabled people's organisations and other civil society organisations in the formulation of PRSP/PEAP in Uganda seemed to have been a function of:

* the experience and preparedness of local disabled people's organisations, NGOs, civil society organisations (CSOs) and individual members of civil society; and
* the willingness of the government to consult and take civil society views into account.

In addition to establishing a unified movement and building consensus among disabled people's organisations, NUDIPU created alliances with the NGO Forum, Combra, Uganda Society for Disabled Children (USDC), Uganda National Institute of Special Education and government departments, particularly the Ministries of Gender Labour and Social Development, Education and Health. NUDIPU also established a working relationship with USAID and World Vision.

NUDIPU's proposals for the PEAP
The process of developing the position paper 'Participation of Organizations and Partners for Persons with Disabilities in the PEAP – 2003 Revision' included reviewing a wide range of literature on disability and poverty in Uganda, interviewing several representatives of DPOs and partners and deliberating at all stakeholders' meetings on the different proposals and options outlined in

proposals (Damurlira 2003).

The position paper pointed out that the former PEAP treated issues about disabled people under the general headings of 'vulnerable groups', 'marginalised groups of society', or 'disadvantaged groups'. However, this kind of grouping had in most cases failed to give explicit strategies and relevant policy interventions for the intended target group(s).

Experience shows that whenever the specific exclusion mechanisms and specific needs of disabled people are not explicitly identified, the related strategies and programmes also miss their specific target. A category like 'vulnerable groups', though useful at certain levels of analysis, becomes an obstacle when it hides essential differences in poverty determinants of various vulnerable subgroups and in strategies required to address their problems. These distinctions are essential even within the category of disabled persons themselves.

In addition to general concerns and issues raised in the position paper, NUDIPU proposed focused interventions that needed to be incorporated in the revised PEAP. These included:

- Pillar I: Creating a framework for economic growth and transformation;
  - public expenditure allocations – medium term and annual – should indicate specific amounts to finance policy interventions for disability;
  - DPOs should be consulted and involved in all planning, design and implementation processes of the PEAP; and
  - formal and informal employment for disabled people should be supported.
- Pillar II: Good governance and security;
  - PEAP should set targets (indicators) to reduce factors that increase the incidence of people becoming impaired – this could be part of the monitoring process, especially that of impairment caused by insecurity;
  - legal systems should recognise and protect the social, economic, political and civil rights of disabled people;
  - there is a need for capacity building of the representatives (councillors) of disabled people in order to improve their capacity to effectively influence processes; and
  - participation and representation of disabled people in decision-making should be extended to tender boards, service commissions, and so on.
- Pillar III: Actions that directly increase the ability of the poor to ease their incomes;

- PEAP should recognise that disabled people need support, such as appropriate skills and technology, as well as access to information;
- disabled people should have access to land; and
- Key agricultural technologies (including technical advice in processing, storage, preservation and so on) to boost their productivity should be made available to disabled agriculturalists.
- Pillar IV: Actions which directly enhance the quality of life;
    - the PEAP needs to provide avenues that enhance accessibility and utilisation of universal primary education (UPE) facilities by disabled children; and
    - besides UPE, it is also important to address education concerns at secondary and other higher institutions.

Furthermore, NUDIPU called for DPOs and government to work out key indicators that could be used to measure progress in poverty reduction among disabled people. The PEAP therefore needed to recognise the involvement of disabled people and DPOs in implementing and monitoring effective progress on poverty reduction in the country.

Problems encountered

CAPACITY CONSTRAINTS

By definition, the countries undertaking PRSPs are both 'heavily indebted' and 'poor'. It is, therefore, inevitable that they will be severely constrained in their capacity to carry out a comprehensive, participatory consultation exercise with all the requirements in terms of personnel/expertise, transport, communications, documentation and so on. Although civil society, if called on to do so, can add to government efforts, it is also true that CSOs and NGOs in a poor country are unlikely to be very well resourced.

The Uganda experience shows that deliberate efforts are needed to build the capacity of DPOs, especially the national organisations, if they are to have greater impact on policy planning, implementation, monitoring and evaluation. Capacity building includes the recruitment of high-calibre, skilled and well-trained staff to implement some of the strategic programmes. Counterparts in government were well trained and knowledgeable and according to our interviewees, often had little patience with the comparatively slow pace on the part of DPOs. At the local level, DPOs need to build the capacity at the grassroots so as to monitor policy implementation. For its part, local government must develop transparent and accountable systems that enable the communities they serve to access the information required to conduct effective monitoring (Africa Budget Watch 2002).

DPOs in Uganda acknowledged that they had their own capacity constraints including insufficient staff, at both national and local level, qualified to engage donors and policy makers in dialogue on macro-economic policy issues. However, they felt that they had much to gain by taking the opportunity offered to participate in the PRSP/PEAP.

The challenges facing the NUDIPU leadership at the time of their participation in the PRSP were:

- the need to provide guidance to the overall process with limited resources and capacity;
- generating and coordinating the views of different components of the disability movement; and
- lobbying for financial support to NUDIPU's participation and concept paper.

Although the disability movement in Uganda did not have the capacity to engage fully or on equal terms in the PRSP/PEAP process, funding from the Danish National Council of Disabled People (DSI) and support from organisations such as Action on Disability and Development (ADD) did play a key role in enabling the movement to develop a good proposal on the needs of disabled people within the PEAP process.

Nonetheless, some respondents recalled that the major difficulty was the lack of clarity on precisely what needs of disabled people should be addressed in the PEAP. Again, it was resource constraints which meant that the movement could not involve local research institutions, which would have significantly helped to overcome this particular problem.

TIME CONSTRAINTS

As noted above, the PRSPs are developed in conditions marked by financial, infrastructural and other capacity constraints. Further, participatory approaches are, by their very nature, long winded as well as expensive. The imposition of, sometimes severe, time constraints on this situation can only make matters worse. It has been noted in the case of Uganda that, 'Process difficulties included the widespread tendency ... to call meetings or make documents available and require civil society to respond at very short notice...' (CIDSE- Caritas 2004)

In the case of the 2005 revision, the pressure was on for the PRSP to be completed as quickly as possible. There was great internal urgency to qualify for debt relief, but this was compounded by external pressure from donors who needed a successful example of a country benefiting from the enhanced HIPC initiative. As a result, the PEAP process, in which civil society had been meaningfully involved, became constricted into a six-month period and DPOs found themselves, to some extent, squeezed out. (African Forum 2002)

The DPOs also had to deal with time pressures and had to distribute their concept paper at every opportunity in order to get buy-in. In addition, the task teams set up to engage government departments had to operate at a very fast pace in order to keep up with developments in the PRSP/PEAP process.

LACK OF SUFFICIENT ACCESS TO INFORMATION

Uganda, more noticeably than other countries, had an active policy of disseminating information about progress on its poverty reduction strategy. This was done through monthly press conferences of leading government officials, regular publications, radio in multiple dialects, special explanatory publications, and indicators to end-users even at the programme level in educational and health facilities. The policy allowed end-users of the programmes to understand what is going on and gauge the success or failure of the programmes

However, for many disabled people this information was inaccessible, not only because of high levels of illiteracy, but also because of the failure to provide materials in different formats. Poverty too limits access to such things as the internet and even television or radio.

DIFFICULTY OF INFLUENCING THE PEAP AGENDA

Another challenge was to be able to use DPO influence to best effect. DPO inputs needed to be mainstreamed into policy planning. However, some government officials still regarded DPO and CSO participation merely as an exercise to legitimise the PRSP process. They still viewed criticism from CSOs with suspicion. Furthermore, DPOs needed to understand fully and analyse the donor agenda. Donors retain a strong influence over budgetary and other policy plans in Africa (and elsewhere in the Third World) because they contribute a large portion of the government budget. For instance, in the financial year 2000/2001, 53% of Uganda's budget was dependent on donors (including loans and grants), while the government contribution was only 47%. (Africa Budget Watch 2002)

On this issue, Pastor Santos Labeja, Vice Chairperson, Uganda National NGO Forum, has commented,

> In Uganda, when civil society was invited to participate in the PRSP, it accepted the invitation with a lot of excitement and expectation. The concepts of 'participation and ownership' are very appealing to civil society. However, it has come to pass that while helping to significantly improve relations between civil society and the Government of Uganda, the 'participation process' has had serious limitations, including reluctance on the part of the World Bank to go all the way with opening up key macroeconomic policies for discussion. (Labeja 2003)

The Outcome – Disability in Uganda's 2005 PEAP/PRSP
As mentioned above, disabled people's organisations were not consulted in the formulation of Uganda's 1997 PEAP or its revision in 2000. As a direct consequence, disability did not figure in either of these plans. One positive outcome of the second revision process was that disability at last appeared and was officially recognised as a major poverty issue. For example, in Chapter 2, 'Poverty in Uganda. Patterns and Trends', it is said that:

> Disabled people suffer relative income poverty in addition to the reduction in their quality of life caused by their disability, the social stigma sometimes experienced, and more limited access to services. In 2000, 46% of persons with disability were poor (using the narrow definition as those who were economically inactive during the last 12 months because of disability), compared to 34% of people in general.

> More information is needed on the extent to which disabled people are able to meet their specific needs such as access to equipment, and the extent to which specific disabilities are currently preventing

economic participation or reducing people's productivity. (Republic of Uganda 2004 p.21)

Disability is also mentioned with respect to making accessible provision in both secondary and higher education, as well as support for community-based rehabilitation (CBR). 'In line with Government's commitment to ensure equitable poverty reduction and in view of the large proportion of PWDs, expansion of community based rehabilitation services (in addition to other mainstreaming interventions) emerges as an issue for priority attention requiring more public intervention.'

While this represents a degree of progress, it falls very far short of what was recommended by NUDIPU in its submission. Furthermore, a recognition of disability is really a rather minor victory, especially when it is remembered that a great many governments and international bodies, including the United Nations, the European Union and the World Bank, have made very strong commitments on mainstreaming disability in development and have done virtually nothing. (see Chapter 4)

Conclusions

Disabled people's participation in the formulation of the PRSP increases democratic ownership of the process. Increased ownership enhances policy implementation so that intended outcomes can be better realised. Whether this happens and the disability movement plays a significant role in future donor-government policy planning processes remains to be seen. What is clear is that for DPOs to influence policies effectively in Uganda and elsewhere in Africa and the developing world, disabled people and their representative organisations must be determined, informed and well-supported. There also needs to be a policy environment, both domestic and international, which is open to their engagement.

It can be argued that to some extent at least two of the three conditions were found in Uganda. The government here did encourage DPO involvement and the disability movement did find support. But, neither the donors themselves nor Ugandan Government have shown a consistent commitment to this principle, particularly in terms of taking into account the most substantive issues raised by the disability movement or allocating adequate fiscal resources to underpin the consultative process.

To be actionable, a long-term vision needs to be embodied in a medium-term strategy that defines goals – with associated roles for the private sector, civil society, local and national governments and external partners – and to be adequately budgeted. As a result of the introduction of the PRSP process, Uganda is among the countries that have developed medium-term development strategies. And while Uganda has achieved some success in aligning its sectoral frameworks with its overall Medium Term Expenditure Framework, there has been no move in the 2005 PEAP document to mainstream disability along the lines proposed by NUDIPU.

One explanation for this is that DPOs were brought into the participatory process, mainly because CSO consultation was required for the PRSP process, not out of a genuine desire to develop a fully inclusive pro-poor development programme. Interestingly, Ugandan CSO involvement more broadly has been held up as a good example of genuine participation. For example, the CIDSE-Caritas background paper found that, 'Uganda provides the only example of more enlightened participation policies, where at the outset government made concrete provision for civil society involvement in monitoring and evaluation of PRS work as well as inputting to the initial PRSP.' (CIDSE-Caritas 2004, p.4) The Ugandan NGO Forum agreed with this, but claimed that participation had little impact on outcomes in that although '…they were invited to provide input on the development of poverty reducing goals (i.e. government expenditure and social policy), they could not participate in the nature of macroeconomic policies to achieve these goals.' They concluded that '…in many ways, participation in PRSPs is engineering consent for structural adjustment policies, a mechanism for cooptation of development activists.' (Labeja 2003)

Broadening the perspective, while Uganda has been touted as a success story of the PRSP process, in terms of the HIPC (Highly Indebted Poor Country) initiative out of which the PRSP was developed, 'After nearly a decade of operation in Uganda, the country still has an unsustainable debt burden. … the IMF/World Bank enforced neo-liberal policies have not brought sustainable development to the economy of Uganda nor support to the country's poverty reduction goals.' (Somerville 2005). This assessment more than holds with respect to disability. In his study on chronic poverty and disability in Uganda, Lwanga-Ntale observes that '…disabled people, as individuals, or the households in which they live, face a kind of poverty condition that carries on for a long period of time - beyond five (5) years, during which period, and regardless of different macro and micro interventions, affected households or individuals are unable to sustain themselves or to improve on their livelihoods.' (Lwanga-

Ntale 2003)

Recommendations

There is much to criticise about how the disability movement has fared in the recent PRSP process. Nonetheless, for the sake of disabled people in the country, it is important to end this summary of our report on a positive note by offering a series of constructive recommendations about how disability can be more effectively included in any subsequent consultative process. To achieve this it is vital that:

* the capacity of DPOs be enhanced substantially, in order to sustain their participation and involvement in the current and future development processes;
* monitoring of PEAP alleviation strategies for disabled people should be based on both qualitative and quantitative approaches, with qualitative studies involving DPO research and study groups, research institutions and other civil society organisations;
* a process of formulating disability indicators and performance benchmarks that cut across key sectors of government, donors, and civil society organisations should be implemented;
* NUDIPU's advocacy for the implementation of legislation and pro-disability poverty alleviation strategies within the PEAP be supported and accelerated with the active involvement of representative organisations that represent different impairment groups;
* ongoing advocacy and lobbying is developed alongside efforts to mainstream disability in all the pillars of the PEAP;
* the government of Uganda should develop appropriate strategies that can address the different needs of different types of disability;
* there is a need to improve information flows to disabled people about their rights. The disability movement should be empowered to advocate for accessible information dissemination strategies on the implementation of government legislation and the PEAP;
* the disability movement should continue to lobby for a share of resources flowing from development cooperation and debt relief. NUDIPU should advocate for budgeting for disability programme components and actual funding allocations to poverty-focused projects that benefit disabled people; and
* NUDIPU should develop capacity to influence development cooperation,

particularly in relation to disability funding policies of agencies that operate in Uganda, such as USAID, DANIDA and NORAD, among others.

References

Africa Budget Watch., 2002 (?). Interview with Zie Gariyo from the Uganda Debt Network. Available at:
http://www.idasa.org.za/gbOutputFiles.asp?WriteContent=Y&RID=1064.

African Forum & Network on Debt and Development., 2002. Civil Society Participation in the Poverty Reduction Strategy Paper (PRSP) Process.

Ambrose, Soren., 2000. Poverty Reduction & Growth: A New Mask for Structural Adjustment. *Economic Justice News,* 3 (3), Available at: http://www.50years.org/cms/ejn/story/150

CIDSE-Caritas., 2004. PRSP: Are the World Bank and IMF delivering on Promises?, International Background Paper. Available at:
http://www.cidse.org/docs/200404221144166307.pdf.

Damurlira, Davis., 2003. Participation of Organisations and Partners for Persons with disabilities in the PEAP 2003 Revision. Report commissioned by NUDIPU, USDC and ADD. Available at:
www.disabilitykar.net/docs/recommendations_nudipu.doc

Disability KaR., 2004. Highlights from Roundtable 1: Poverty, Development and the Millennium Development Goals. November. Available at:
http://www.disabilitykar.net/roundtables/malawi_rt.html

Labeja, Santos., 2003. Poverty Monitoring And Evaluation By Civil Society: Uganda Case. Uganda National NGO Forum. June. Available at:
http://www.cspr.org.zm/Reports&Updates/UgandaPresentation.doc

Nyamugasira, Warren and Rowden, Rick., 2002. New Strategies, Old Loan Conditions. Do the New IMF and World Bank Loans Support Countries' Poverty Reduction Strategies? The Case of Uganda, Action Aid. Available at:
http://www.internationalbudget.org/resources/library/UgandaPRSP.pdf

Okidi, John A., Ssewanyana, Sarah, Bategeka, Lawrence and Muhumuza, Fred., 2004. Operationalising Pro-Poor Growth. A Joint Initiative of AFD, BMZ, (GTZ, KfW development Bank), DFID and the World Bank. Kampala: Economic Policy Research Centre. October. Available at: http://www.dfid.gov.uk/pubs/files/oppguganda.pdf

Piron, Laure-Hélène with Norton, Andy., 2004. Politics and the PRSP Approach: Uganda Case Study. Working Paper 240. London: Overseas Development Institute. March.

Republic of Uganda, Ministry of Finance., 2004. Planning and Economic Development, *Poverty Eradication Action Plan (2004/5 – 2007/8),* Kampala.

Somerville, Richie., 2005. Evaluation Of The Operation Of The Heavily Indebted Poor Country (HIPC) Initiative In Uganda. *Student Economic Review.* 19. Available at: http://www.tcd.ie/Economics/SER/archive/2005/18sommerville.pdf

CHAPTER 11

Capacity building with Dpos in Mozambique

Jabulani Ncube

This chapter is written from the perspective of disabled people who have been at the receiving end of externally-driven capacity building initiatives. Because the essential assumption underlying capacity building is that it is 'good for them', and helps to facilitate local actors to build the skills and tools necessary to take control and drive their own development initiatives, it is crucial for those providing the capacity building to listen carefully to the voices of the presumed beneficiaries in order to understand how the process is playing out in practice.

The aim of the research was to give life to these voices by examining the role and efficacy of DPO capacity-building initiatives in Mozambique. This was done by comparing and contrasting the approaches of Northern DPOs and IN-GOs who are active in disability and development in that country. The principal outcome hoped for was to be able to identify the most effective approaches and why they have worked.

The research was carried out during two brief visits to the country in the first half of 2005. Information was gathered through semi-structured interviews, a questionnaire and a workshop for DPOs. Five local DPOs were surveyed, including FAMOD (Forum for Mozambican Associations of Disabled People), the national umbrella organization of all associations of disabled people. With respect to the Northern-based organisations, two were International NGOs (KEPA – Service Centre for Development Cooperation (Finland) and POWER (UK)) run by non-disabled people and two were DPOs based in Finland (FIDIDA - International Development Association of Disabled Persons and the ABILIS Foundation).

As researcher, I see my role as that of an intermediary who was available to articulate the perspective of DPOs in Mozambique. That I have been a member of and worked with DPOs in Africa for nearly 30 years accords me a unique opportunity to convey their message and interpret it within an experiential framework as well as a broader theoretical structure.

Disability in Mozambique

The situation facing disabled people in Mozambique is largely representative of disabled people living in other poor developing countries, except that Mozambique is an extraordinarily poor country. According to the UNDP (2004), it ranked 171st out of 177 countries, with a Human Development Index of 0.354, compared with Seychelles, which ranked first in the same region, with an index of 0.853, and sitting at 35th position world wide. In the same UNDP (2004) report, Mozambique ranks 89th among 95 developing countries in terms of the Human Poverty Index.

Mozambique does have a disability policy, but it remains unimplemented. With the support of the POWER a plan of action had been drafted to help with the implementation of the policy. However, in contrast with the growing trend for such laws in the region, there is no specific legislation on disability. The Ministry of Women and Social Action is the government body charged with the responsibility of overseeing disability issues, but as will be explained below, it is vastly under funded. Besides the Ministry, the other main actors in disability are:

- FAMOD – the national umbrella organisation of more than a dozen DPOs; and
- the main foreign donors are KEPA, FIDIDA and the ABILIS Foundation, all from Finland, and POWER from the UK.

Key issues facing disabled people in Mozambique

During the consultations many similarities in the nature of issues confronting disabled people were identified by the DPOs themselves, by both their Northern NGO and DPO partners, and by the Ministry of Women and Social Action. These included:

- extreme levels of poverty. The long anti-colonial struggle, and the post-independence civil war between FRELIMO and RENAMO helped to exacerbate poverty in general, increasing the prevalence of disabling impairment in the process;
- very low levels of education and illiteracy;
- lack of income and employment opportunities;
- low self-esteem;
- unstable membership bases of DPOs, due to unmet basic needs of members;
- The gap between leaders and ordinary members (which reduces the ef-

fectiveness of DPOs as representatives of the wider constituency);
* little involvement of disabled women in training activities; and
* the need for the disability movement to be decentralised away from
  Maputo to the outlying, rural areas. The growing focus on the provinces is
  seen as a challenging opportunity for FAMOD in terms of the requirement
  to co-ordinate with provincial structures, as well as to share information
  with them.

Making all the above more problematic is the fact that there is limited funding
available for the disability sector and there are so few external donors. The result
is that DPOs are over-dependent on the few NGOs that are involved, mainly the
Finnish organisations and POWER. Despite there being so few foreign donors,
DPOs felt there is a lack of effective sharing and comparing of notes and plans
among them. This often had a negative impact on the DPOs. For example, they
were often called upon to engage in similar training activities by different agencies. This not only wasted scarce resources as well as the time of DPOs, but also
led to considerable confusion.

To make matters even worse, the Ministry of Women and Social Action, the
lead ministry charged with overseeing disability issues, is grossly under-funded
and also expects funding from the same foreign agencies that support the disability sector. This is a cause of considerable anxiety among DPOs, who see
the real possibility of the interests of the Ministry and theirs clashing, as they
both scramble for funding from the same sources. With the Ministry's dire need
for funding came the possibility of Northern INGOs agreeing separate arrangements with it, outside of any agreements they might have with the disability
movement. DPOs interpret this as denying necessary resources to them, as they
do not get any funding from the government. This analysis finds support in the
fact that KEPA has decided that from 2006 onwards instead of working through
the Ministry it will work directly with civil society organisations, including
DPOs.

Another problem is having a relatively under-funded ministry taking the
lead over disability issues. This lessens its influence with other government
ministries while at the same time allowing these ministries to avoid doing
anything about disability, arguing that it is not their responsibility. This raises
the question of where disability issues should be located in government for
maximum influence. The Africa Decade Continental Plan of Action advises that
this needs to be considered for locating either in the Office of the President,

as it does in South Africa, or the Office of the Prime Minister, where the latter exists. Despite the question of competition for funds and other difficulties, in what can be seen as a generally weak policy environment concerning disability, there is an opportunity for DPOs to advocate in favour of new policies and programmes at government and civil society levels. For example, there is a need for government support to DPOs, to increase access to social services for disabled people, improve the education of disabled children and include disability in HIV/AIDS programmes of other organizations. However, besides the chronic lack of resources, the fragile unity among DPOs remains a major problem, undermining disabled people's ability to have a sufficiently authoritative political voice.

Resulting impacts on disabled people and their organisations
Given the situation facing disabled people described in the foregoing section, the impact of this can be summarised as follows:

- the ability of DPO leaders to network effectively and relate with other organisations is limited by low levels of education, including their difficulty in organising members and assertively influence policy makers and other key players in the disability field. In the light of these problems, to have established a network of organizations which unite efforts at the national level under the umbrella of FAMOD, is a considerable achievement;
- the gap between policy makers and disabled people is considerable and effectively keeps the majority of disabled people disconnected from the major, city-based DPOs. This is to a large degree due to gaps in knowledge, skills and language;
- the dominant image of disabled people as beggars militates against their ability to assert themselves as advocates of their cause and to be taken seriously; and
- there are difficulties to be faced in working with all poor people facing daily challenges to meet basic needs. The 'charity ethic' was described as running deep among the majority of disabled people in Mozambique. Expectations of, and indeed the need for, immediate, tangible benefits constitutes a constraint that needs to be considered in all interventions with poor disabled people.

Mozambican perspectives on organisational capacity building for DPOs

One key method of starting to address the deep-seated problems faced by disabled people in Mozambique is to strengthen their organisations. It was said by disabled people who were surveyed that they conceive capacity building as a process that enables them to acquire 'legs with which to walk'. This underlines a fundamental perception and belief in the role of their organizations. These are seen as the means to drive a process of change aimed at benefiting disabled people. As such, disabled people's organizations represent a significant social movement (Oliver, 1990).

The capacity to initiate and sustain change is anchored in a belief in the soundness of their philosophical grounding, and the efficacy and nature of the vehicle through which that grounding is expressed. At the same time, it is recognised that disabled people must be in the forefront of efforts to drive change from which they ultimately benefit. Their own organizations provide the instrumentality for that change to be systematically addressed. The legitimacy of their organizations can only be maintained if they are able to remain relevant to the practical and strategic needs of their constituencies.

From the aforementioned perspective, development agencies wishing to support disabled people need to decide how they conceive the modalities of progressive economic and social transformation. Are they going to help disabled people deepen their own understanding of what needs to change? Are they going to help them build and strengthen their own groups and organizations in order to work effectively for this change? Above all, are they willing to learn from disabled people and their struggles?

In Mozambique, disabled people have invested considerable time and energy in developing their own structures and it is, therefore, easier and more effective for an outsider to find a home for their interventions within these structures. But if an external agency adopts a top-down approach, does not really trust disabled people or what they are seeking to achieve, the latter's organisations may then be seen as little more than an 'opportunist' entry point for financing a short-term project or two, while ignoring the longer-term commitment that is required. It is key that any outside interventions must '...allow the poor, weak and vulnerable to express their realities, to plan, to act...It is astonishing that it has taken so long...for the development community...to discover not just the richness of the knowledge of local people, but more crucially their creative and analytical abilities' (Chambers 1997, pp. 103&128).

I refer to the longer-term engagement with DPOs because it is important to understand that capacity building efforts aimed at creating effective people's organizations require precisely such a perspective and commitment of resources. In his report assessing the impact of Comic Relief's long-term support for the disability sector in Uganda, Peter Macfadyen states 'This is by far the largest portfolio of disability grants made by Comic Relief in one country (19 grants worth £3.5 million). It is also one of the longest consistent periods of support around the same issue in any grants programme [of Comic Relief]....And it includes a steady flow of support for rights-based work....With such a range of work, over a long period of time, it is possible to make some comparisons in relation to the effectiveness of inputs.' (Macfadyen 2005). The alternative approach of brief entry and exit constitutes unacceptable interference in people's lives and represents no meaningful socio-political solidarity with their broader struggle for dignity, human rights and social transformation.

In development cooperation more widely, the language of partnership has been recycled for over two decades. It is also apparent that the sides of this particular road are littered with the bleached skeletons of failed partnerships. Furthermore, many of the existing ones are on the rocks, to the extent that to continue calling them genuine or productive partnerships borders on undisguised exaggeration at best and at worst a total fiction. In this respect, the message from disabled Mozambicans indicates a need to rethink the nature of the alliances which are required between their organizations and those who wish to work in partnership with them.

The Mozambican DPOs are clear that an important outcome of capacity building should enable them to identify potential allies and seek meaningful dialogue with them. Secondly, they want to be able to increase their ability to identify the needs of both their organizations and their members, while strengthening their ability to be effective in addressing those needs. The question which they suggested had to be asked continually is 'How are we using the resources and capacity of our organization to benefit the membership?' (Tembe, FAMOD Secretary General/Coordinator) There is, however, the recognition by DPOs that each of the organizations have differing levels of capacity. This attests once again to the long-term nature of the challenges they face on the road to effectiveness and sustainability.

An area identified for close examination by the DPOs, because of its potential opportunities to increase their effectiveness, relates to building relationships with other national DPOs, and opening new lines along which cooperation could be built. Experience within SAFOD (Southern African Federation of the Disabled) suggests that cooperation and information sharing among DPOs within the region has been valuable. Commonality of experiences, perspectives and issues facing the disability movement demonstrates the need for not only South-South cooperation, but also that South-North-South linkages require to be deepened. This has been demonstrated through experience gained by many DPOs within the global disability movement, represented by DPI (Disabled People's International).

Different approaches in supporting capacity building
We turn now to a brief discussion of the impact of varying operating methods of donors on DPOs in Mozambique. The findings are based on interviews and workshops carried out during the research, more details of which can be found in the full report.

It was clear in our discussions with members of DPOs that they experienced a number of problems working with POWER. These arose because of the absence of a commonly-shared vision about the goals their DPO partners were pursuing, as well as the objectives for attaining them. The difficulties DPOs cited were inflexibility in negotiating plans and allocating funds for their implementation. A 'take it or leave it' attitude on POWER's part would appear to reflect insensitivity, suggesting an unwillingness to engage in open and frank dialogue. DPOs accused POWER of not paying attention to their needs. This left them feeling they had become involved in a markedly unequal and disempowering relationship.

POWER directly administers the financial arrangements relating to training activities they support, even if the local DPO partner often has to undertake a range of local activities such as contacting participants, travelling and other logistics associated with preparation of the planned activity.

In contrast, the Finnish INGO, KEPA appeared to understand the need for a multi-pronged approach to capacity building. In addition to training inputs, they allowed FAMOD a level of flexibility in programme and project implementation by providing funding towards a FAMOD defined budget which included elements of some key core costs. Once the budget was funded, FAMOD exercised control over implementation, while understanding their ultimate accountability to KEPA in terms of providing periodic narrative and financial reports. This flexible arrangement was acknowledged to have contributed to building other important skills for the organisation in the areas of budget planning and management, improved organizational administrative procedures and report writing. In addition it promoted accountability, transparency and good organizational governance. FAMOD's participation in KEPA's strategic planning exercise was acknowledged to have greatly helped FAMOD to develop their own strategic plan.

For reasons explained above, the relationship FAMOD had with KEPA was perceived by FAMOD as being empowering, trusting and was understood to be building towards a more power-balanced partnership. KEPA, nevertheless, saw that a certain power asymmetry existed, which would tend to prevail in their favour given that they carried the 'cheque book'.

While the foregoing discussion has focussed on relationships between the umbrella organization and its member DPOs with both POWER and KEPA, the following briefly examines the relationships DPOs in Mozambique were building with their Northern DPO partners in both the UK and Finland.

DPOs in the North shared much in common with their counterpart DPOs in Mozambique, due to the shared understanding of the issues involved in building organizations of disabled people. FAMOD had enjoyed a close working relationship with both FIDIDA and ABILIS of Finland. Experiences and views were shared more honestly. An example was given by FAMOD relating to the close mutual understanding of how issues of poverty among disabled people in Mozambique affected the extent of their participation in DPO activities. Secondly, some challenges such as the geographic spread of members posed difficulties with communication. Yet because DPOs are supposed to be membership organizations, the organizational structures made it essential that reach was extended across the country, to the extent that resources allowed. These challenges were said to be more empathetically understood among the DPOs themselves, Northern and Mozambican.

Further examples of how DPO-DPO relationships have been perceived include an observation by Mozambicans that their Northern DPO partners have been less imposing, that they have shown more willingness to listen and be flexible in their mutual dealings. To this extent, their Northern DPO partners have been understood to be less complicated to deal with than the non-disabled-led INGOs. The commonly shared experience of disability is understood by the Mozambican DPOs to provide a basis for building long-term relationships with their Northern counterparts.

It is important that the DPO is recognized as the driver of the process of capacity building as this is closely related to the ability of the DPO to continue its engagement with development issues relevant to its members beyond the exit of the external partner. Because DPOs represent their members, however poorly this may work in practice due to a host of reasons (some of which have been outlined) to ignore their own understanding of their capacity needs is tantamount to denying their legitimacy.

To underpin DPOs' ability to drive the process, training is obviously vital, but it needs to act as a 'trigger' to kick-start action. This was why DPO members placed such emphasis on the need for resourcing their organisations to put into practice the skills that had been acquired. If this is not done, training will be, in effect, 'training for nothing', as one participant in the consultative workshop characterized it. Failing to follow up results in a loss of opportunities, occasions frustration and leads to the evaporation of the knowledge and skills acquired.

Another criticism of training was that northern NGOs relied almost exclusively on relatively high-waged imported capacity-building experts from the north. This is illustrative of the concept some of them seem to hold of the development processes as being made up of technical interventions best left to experts, who invariably happen to exclude from their ranks disabled people themselves. If capacity building is about building sustainable capacities in organizations of local people, then respecting and valuing the agency of disabled people is a critical matter in utilising their organizations to achieve long term social change, much like what David Booth refers to as 'micro-foundations of the macro-framework' (Booth 1994, p.13.)

Building strong DPOs has a wider social and political purpose. The image and profile of disabled people's organizations in the public domain is an important issue, as they engage through advocacy and networking with the policy process. It is this work which increases the visibility of disability issues, while challenging public attitudes to disability. Such visibility has additionally served to cascade the organizations' work upwards into the national arena. Experiences of national disability movements in Uganda, Namibia and South Africa, to name only a few countries, provides evidence of how the work of the movement essentially 'scales up' its impact. Members of Parliament representing the constituency of disabled people, at least in some of these countries, have arrived at such positions as a result of direct lobbying by disabled people through their organizations and has thus led to recognition by national leaderships of the need for such representation at different levels of governance, including national parliaments. Belief in the efficacy of DPOs by disabled people, coupled with the abiding support of their Northern allies, as has happened in some cases, vindicates the longer-term investment made in and the trust given to these organizations. 'Politics matter for human development because people everywhere want to be free to determine their destinies, express their views and participate in the decisions that shape their lives' (UNDP 2002, p.1).

Disabled people, through their organizations, are not demanding to take over of INGOs or the role of governments, but to be listened to and taken seriously.

> It is good for them to know, the gentlemen of money, that the times of yesterday will no longer be those of today nor those of tomorrow....They shall no longer humiliate those of us who are the colour of the earth. We have always had a voice. But it shall no longer be a murmur which lowers its head. It shall now be a shout which lifts the gaze and we shall force them to see us as we are, and to accept us as we are. Subcomandante Marcos. (Gaia network undated)

In Mozambique DPOs are saying that they should not to be treated as clients and objects of capacity building. They wish to have partners who support them by genuinely listening and who allow them space to discuss their issues and formulate strategies to address them. They want assistance to occupy a frontline position in order to take the necessary decisions themselves. Paternalistic forms of relationships fall far short of this goal, while at the same time failing to legitimate the experience or abilities of disabled people. Existing organizational weaknesses should be the basis for the offer of appropriate capacity building support and not be used to condemn DPOs out of hand as being incapable.

Conclusion

It is important to indicate some important limitations of making broader generalisations based on the Mozambican case study. While the following conclusions are important, it is necessary that the reader understands this was only a single short-term study in one country. Nevertheless, it does represents issues that DPOs elsewhere in Southern and East Africa would perhaps recognize, to a greater or lesser extent, as relevant to them.

The key conclusions of this chapter are several. Disabled people view their organizations as serving the vital function of providing them with unifying power to make their voices heard. It is important for any intervention to recognize this strategic role that disabled people expect from their organisations.

As socio-political movements, they represent a vehicle for change that is in the hands of their members. It is obviously of considerable importance that the capacity of this vehicle is nurtured. Further, the organizations represent a part of the partnership for change that has to be negotiated and secured with government, civil society and international development agencies.

Secondly, despite their protestations to the contrary, there are some INGOs that do not see the DPO project in the South for what it is. They may work with it but at the same time cannot really accept its desire for greater autonomy or the need for them to let go of the reins. Doing that would threaten their power, salaries and benefits, even their very reason to exist. Most national DPOs, as well as the international movement represented by DPI, were born in the process of resistance against the paternalistic oppression exercised by groups that claimed to speak for them. Disabled people's organizations will pay a heavy price if they forget this aspect of the struggle in which they have been engaged. It persists and still poses a threat to disabled people's desire for justice and equality.

Closely related to the last point is that access to Northern resources is through channels that are controlled by the disability movement's 'strategic' opponents. I am, of course, not painting all agencies with the same brush, but it should not be underestimated how costly this arrangement has been to disabled people's organizations. A 'broker' is an expensive method of doing business. Experience indicates that the brokered relationship has short changed the disability movement, by acting as a fine sieve, which allows only minute particles to trickle down to those at the bottom. The balance of power is clearly tilted to the side of the powerful INGOs. This can be seen if we consider over the years whose capacity has been strengthened more by this relationship, the INGOs or the Southern DPOs? The disability movement must consider alternative routes to obtain the required resources, as the Mozambican experience attests to the need to seek change in this essentially unequal power relationship.

Fourth, capacity building through training activities is not the only way to increase the effectiveness of people and their organizations. The Mozambicans have emphasized the need, following training inputs, for them to be given an opportunity to practice what they have learnt. However, funds to do exactly this are hard to come by from their partners. DPOs have suggested flexibility in negotiating expenditure of funds with their partners and the priorities to which those funds should be allocated. They have also suggested increased utilization of local and regionally-sourced expertise, rather than almost invariably relying on Northern 'experts'.

Fifth, the limits of effectiveness faced by the Ministry of Women and Social Action, is symptomatic of many government bodies in different countries which are tasked to oversee disability issues. They invariably tend to be underfunded for their role to be discharged effectively. As a consequence they have limited capacity and knowledge of disability issues and, therefore, an inability to influence other ministries and state bodies. Furthermore, individuals with knowledge of and commitment to disability who they might have in their ranks tend to move to better opportunities as a result of the constraints within which they have to work. The recommendation of the Africa Decade Continental Plan of Action, suggesting that consideration be given to locating disability issues in the office either of the state President or the Prime Minister, as the case may be, stems from this analysis. The logic of the recommendation is that agencies linked to the highest office in the land stand a better chance of competing for limited funds.

Finally, the lack of effective collaboration among different Northern NGOs which support DPOs promotes unnecessary duplication, waste of resources and confusion with their DPO partners. This is a luxury that disabled people in the South cannot afford.

References

Booth, D., 1994. Rethinking social development: theory, research and practice. In D. Booth, D. ed. *Rethinking social development: an overview.* Harlow: Longman Scientific & Technical.

Chambers R., 1997. *Whose Reality Counts: putting the first last.* London: Intermediate Technology Publications.

Gaia network, undated. Zapatistas. Online. Available at: http://home.clara.net/heureka/gaia/zapatistas.htm

Macfadyen, P., 2005. Learning Trip (To test hypothesis that 'A strong rights based component to development inputs is essential for long term positive change in the lives of disabled people. Unpublished Mss. Disabled People's Programme, COMIC RELIEF, UK.

Oliver, M., 1990. *The Politics of Disablement,* Basingstoke: Macmillan and St Martin's Press.

UNDP., 2002. Human Development Report 2002: deepening democracy in a fragmented world. New York: Oxford University Press.

United Nations Development Programme, 2004. *Human Development Report 2004*. New York: Oxford University Press.

CHAPTER 12

Disability in conflict and emergency situations: Focus on tsunami-affected areas

Victor Cordeiro, Shivaram Deshpande, Maria Kett, Sue Stubbs and Rebecca Yeo

On 26th December 2004, a tsunami in the Indian Ocean hit coastal regions of South Asia and East Africa from Thailand to Somalia. Almost 200,000 people were killed, and more than a million displaced, together with huge destruction of livelihoods and infrastructure. The scale of the public response around the world was unprecedented. By December 2005, $6.1billion had been donated – more than two thirds coming from individuals and NGOs.(Reliefweb & Reality of Aid) For once emergency response organisations were not dealing with insufficient resources. For once, there was over-abundance.

The tsunami was not a typical disaster in many ways. High levels of funding and media interest resulted in some areas being over funded, competition between funding agencies and pressure to show results visible to the donating public. As a result of the tsunami, many people were killed outright. There was not, therefore, a large increase in numbers of people with impairments. Meanwhile, statistical evidence on numbers of disabled people affected by the tsunami is vague and unreliable. Many testimonies from disabled people describe losing families, homes and livelihoods as well as mobility aids, medicines and support structures.

Research by the International Disability and Development Consortium (IDDC) examined the extent and manner in which disabled people are included in the response to emergency situations, looking particularly at the response to the tsunami in Sri Lanka, India and to a lesser extent in Indonesia. Several member organisations of the Consortium contributed to the work. The aim of the research was to promote the inclusion of disability, both through the methodology and through dissemination of the research results. Readers are referred to the full research report for a more detailed description of findings.

Extent of inclusion

Indian researchers reported some inclusion of disabled people in the distribution of relief materials, aids and appliances. In Sri Lanka, several organisations of and for disabled people were involved in lobbying for disabled people's needs to be considered in the reconstruction. But the research found little evidence of disabled people being included in agenda setting or decision making regarding the tsunami or post-conflict reconstruction in Sri Lanka or India.

Disability is rarely a priority for mainstream agencies, but Action Aid India was found to be an exception. It has a policy that 10 per cent of total resources should be allocated to disabled people and all capacity building and training materials should include disabled people. Their training manual on disaster preparedness also refers to the need to include disabled people. However, in general there was found to be a mismatch between official responses and the reality of limited participation.

Some INGOs claim to include disabled people, but this is usually on the basis of them being a 'vulnerable' group, with 'special needs', rather than understanding the need for mainstreaming disability. This is consistent with the fact that few organisations seem to consider how disabled people can participate in mainstream activities. For example, in Sri Lanka, 'cash-for-work' schemes are currently the only source of work for many people, but disabled people have been virtually excluded from taking part.

OXFAM, a leading INGO, would seem to be promoting, at least on paper, genuine inclusion. In 2003 they published a training manual, 'Disability, Equality, and Human Rights' (Harris and Enfield 2003), which lays out in some detail how to develop and manage inclusive projects. However, their staff in the tsunami-hit regions had had no specific training on disability issues. For example, OXFAM was involved in building latrines several feet off the ground (because of the high water table post tsunami), but had not thought to provide ramps. In one of the organisation's offices, staff acknowledged that if they came across disabled people in the camps they generally referred them onto specialist organisations such as Handicap International (HI) rather than include them in their general programmes.

This kind of behaviour is seemingly at odds with the fact that there has been a noticeable change in language used by development agencies in recent years. However, on closer examination their behaviour is entirely consistent. This is because while specialist disability and international development organisations consulted during this research make some mention of commitment to the social model of disability in their promotional materials, there appears to be widespread confusion as to what this means. Furthermore, many specialist disability agencies were founded on medical-model approaches. Whilst they may now use terms such as the 'social model' and 'inclusion', in reality they maintain a strong focus on impairments rather than disabling barriers or issues around discrimination and human rights. Language such as 'crippled by polio', 'crawling in the dirt', and the implication that rehabilitation is the saviour, is found on websites of agencies claiming to operate within the social model. Evidence of genuine inclusion was rare.

'It seems that the majority of development agencies have misunderstood the concept of inclusion - ignoring focussed interventions on the pretext that special attention may result in exclusion.' (Despande and Cordeiro 2005)

In comparison to the INGOs, Local organisations tend to have fewer policies regarding disability inclusion, but among the small sample involved in this research, staff were in fact more receptive to discussion of inclusion issues than the staff of international organisations.

Not all INGOs conformed to this pattern. MERLIN, an international charity specialising in medical relief for those effected by disasters, was working to improve access to health facilities and had requested training on inclusive practice from Access for All, a consortium of disability organisations, including Spinal Injuries Association Sri Lanka, Motivation and John Grooms, set up shortly after the tsunami (Access for All nd.) .

Consultation, Participation and Representation

The terms 'participation' and 'consultation' are widely used in the international development sector. However, the inherent power issues are rarely acknowledged. The power, status, and financial backing of international organisations mean that under-funded local organisations often 'agree' to participate in an agenda which at core is not their own. Researchers attended consultation meetings in which participants were asked what they thought of reconstruction ideas without any discussion of possible alternatives or priorities. Moreover, unless local DPOs have a proven track record, it is often difficult for them to be considered as a serious partnership option by the lead agencies. This does not auger well for relatively inexperienced DPOs.

There were two networks lobbying for accessible reconstruction in Sri Lanka after the tsunami: 'Access for All' and 'Development with Disabled'. This work included disabled people, but both networks were set up by international organisations. There is a danger that if aid agencies are lobbied by non-disabled Europeans this can be misinterpreted as consultation with local disabled people. If non-disabled people are perceived as speaking on behalf of disabled people it reinforces the idea that disabled people are incapable of speaking for themselves.

Several of the most active members of the Sri Lanka coalition of disability organisations, the Disability Organisations Joint Front (DOJF), are highly educated English-speaking men living in Colombo who became disabled later in life. These people relate well to the staff of international organisations and government. However, their lives are far removed from rural-based disabled people affected by conflict or the tsunami. The issue is whether or not they legitimately represent disabled people in other contexts. Indeed, is a poor disabled person affected by the tsunami automatically a representative of others living in this situation, or does representation depend more on being receptive to other's views and specifically being asked to represent them? Debates about representation are not new, there are no simple answers, but the complexity needs to be understood, otherwise many people will remain invisible. As Cordeiro and Deshpande (2005) discovered when working on this research in India:

> The need for coordination is of course true in relation to ensuring that the whole disabled community is included, but this is extremely challenging for under-resourced, small-scale DPOs and disability NGOs in an emergency response situation, and feedback from disabled people in these situations indicates lack of coordination and information sharing, resulting in increased isolation and neglect of particularly vulnerable groups such as those with intellectual impairment, disabled women, and children

The participants (including the disabled people) in this research cannot represent all disabled people. There are inevitably differences in opinions and needs, based on personalities, gender, age, ethnic, class and geographical differences.

Whose agenda is being implemented?

The Sri Lankan government taskforce on reconstruction, TAFREN, was established immediately after the tsunami. It is composed entirely of business leaders, many with no previous experience of emergency situations. Critics say it is being used to push through the needs of big business at the expense of the needs of ordinary people affected by the tsunami.(MONLAR 2005). Many similarities have been found between the TAFREN agenda and the previously rejected World Bank Poverty Reduction Strategy Paper (PRSP). In 2002 the Sri Lankan government published 'Regaining Sri Lanka' (Government of Sri Lanka 2002). This included many of the economic reforms common to PRSPs around the world, such as privatisation and tax reduction. The paper called for public-private partnerships to upgrade such sectors as water, ports and transportation. It also called for the establishment of large-scale tourism development zones for high-potential tourist areas and for 'immediate action to acquire the land'. There were major protests over the introduction of the PRSP (EURODAD 2003). National elections brought in a new coalition government, promising not to continue such policies.

The TAFREN plans contained $150m of infrastructure development, including areas that were not affected by the tsunami, such as Colombo. The Movement for National Land and Agricultural Reform (MONLAR) points out that, 'The tsunami has provided massive international financial support, but the plans prepared by the Government clearly show that they give much higher priority to carrying out their previous plans as agreed earlier with the international financial institutions' (MONLAR 2005).

Part of the PRSP had called for public-private partnership in water supply: 'In the rural areas...the cost of maintaining and operating systems will be born by the community. In towns and urban areas private sector will be encouraged. Water has an economic value and 'Users should...bear the recurrent costs of drinkingwater' (MONLAR 2005). In Sri Lanka more than 90% of disabled people earn less than $2 a day. 99% of people with an intellectual impairment and 75% of people with mobility impairment are unemployed (Ministry of Social Welfare 2003). Disabled people are clearly amongst the poorest of the poor. Having to pay for such an essential commodity as water clearly has potentially devastating consequences for the poorest, including disabled people. On 30th December 2004 (four days after the tsunami), the Government got Cabinet approval for a water resources policy and a draft bill to legalize the privatisation of water.

The Water Supply and Drainage and the Telecom sector of TAFREN (led by Rajan Brito, director of Aitken Spence, a tourism and logistic company) appeared to be taking no account of disabled people's access needs. A representative of this sector claimed that as only 1% of the population is disabled, providing accessible water supplies for disabled people was not a great concern.

Meanwhile, Hazel Jones from the Water Engineering and Development

Centre at Loughborough University (WEDEC) visited Sri Lanka in 2005 to work with Access for All helping ensure that the reconstructed water and sanitation systems are physically accessible to disabled people. WEDEC have done considerable work to design ways to make water and sanitation systems accessible to disabled people. Easily understandable diagrams of how to design such systems should make the job easier for builders of new systems. Of course all water and sanitation systems should be built in ways that are accessible to all. Whilst such work could be applauded, it is not without its dangers. Protests have taken place in Sri Lanka about the potential privatisation of water system. Protesters are not predominantly disabled people and the issue is not primarily about physical access, but financial access. If water were privatised then many disabled people would not be able to afford it, regardless of whether or not the pumps are physically accessible. Moreover, designing physically accessible water systems could actually be a way for the increasingly notorious private water companies to gain some vestiges of credibility. This example highlights the dangers of campaigning on issues in isolation.

Inclusion in whose agenda? The politics of access and inclusion
Inclusion is frequently talked about as if it were a neutral term. But there are conflicting agendas into which inclusion could be sought. It seems that rather than discuss the merits of the different agendas, disability-specific NGOs were lobbying for inclusion into the agenda of the establishment.

Herman Kumara, head of the National Fisheries Solidarity Movement in Negombo, refers to the reconstruction in Sri Lanka as 'a plan of action amidst the tsunami crisis to hand over the sea and the coast to foreign corporations and tourism, with military assistance from the US Marines.' (Klein 2005). The leaders of the tourist sector of TAFREN were keen to establish a dialogue on making the reconstruction of the tourist infrastructure physically accessible to disabled people. Whilst fishing communities and their allies (MONLAR 2005) are demonstrating against this potential destruction of their livelihoods and construction of a 'paradise for tourism and big business' (TAFREN 2005a), the Access for All campaign has been working with TAFREN to push for physical accessibility in the rebuilding of the hotels. Some foreign tourists may gain from the accessible hotels, but as over 90 per cent of disabled Sri Lankans have an income of less than $2 a day (Ministry of Social Welfare 2003), only a small minority of local disabled people could have financial access to these hotels. Some local disabled people may gain employment in the reconstructed tourist industry, if wider discrimination is addressed. However, many from among the poorest communities would lose their livelihoods in the process. Unless physical access is combined with financial and social access, then it becomes at best meaningless and at worst gives credibility to policies that may benefit the foreign tourist market but are deeply destructive to the local community.

The development agenda in which disabled people are to be included rarely seems to be questioned. The World Bank makes great efforts in its rhetoric to be seen to be working more inclusively. However, in Sri Lanka, community organisations were demonstrating against the impact that the World Bank and other International Financial Institutions (IFIs) on the reconstruction agenda. Those lobbying for disability access may focus so exclusively on disability at the expense of working with others in similar positions of marginalisation and exclusion that they are unable to see the bigger picture. B. Venkatesh, a disabled activist in India has noted:

I find I am in a cocoon with similar beings – disabled people and the professionals who work with them. I say 'cocoon' because... we insulate ourselves from the outside world. We think, plan and implement campaign issues on disability and nothing else. We are so insulated that we do not see that issues like structural adjustment, liberalisation, global warming etc have grave implications for us. We live in a world of our own....We form, at best, 10 per cent of the world's population. Much of our problem is from the other 90 per cent. We need them more than they need us.... Our strength is in our numbers: 10 per cent is too small for us to be of any consequence as a vote bank, especially because we are not organised in countries like (India). The more we become visible and actively engaged in mainstream development issues the greater is the chance of disability getting on to the agenda of development strategy. Another major reason for such active engagement is to protect our environment and to protect the interest of poor people including poor disabled people. (Venkatesh 2004)

Many aid workers, locals and expatriates, claim to be apolitical in their work. This may be in order to maintain good relations with government and because of limitations of charitable status in some countries. But neutrality is impossible and lack of assessment of the political context can reduce the humanitarian impact. Furthermore, the rhetoric of disability access could also be used to give credibility to an agenda that is destructive of the poor community as a whole, including disabled people.

Mental health and psychosocial issues

Sri Lanka has one of the highest rates of suicide in the world. Possible factors contributing to this include conflict, unemployment and poverty (WHO nd). Anecdotally, since the tsunami, rates of suicide and of mental illness have become even higher. Basic Needs was a partner NGO in this research and works to address mental health issues. Since the tsunami, 'psychosocial support' has become an issue of much more widespread concern among NGOs. According to the Consortium of Humanitarian Agencies (nd) in Sri Lanka there were currently 45 registered organisations offering psychosocial support compared to 35 offering more general health support. There did seem to be much greater acceptance of mental health issues caused by the trauma of the tsunami than of longer-term ongoing issues.

Despite this, discrimination on the basis of mental illness is rife. In one hospital visited, a man with a fractured femur was denied treatment due to his 'mental illness'. The man had a supportive family and was able to look after himself. However, his consultant felt it was not feasible to stop his medication in order to undertake an operation. Instead, the man was provided with a wheelchair and discharged home.

One psychiatrist interviewed felt that the tsunami may be a catalyst for the Ministry of Health to improve mental health services. This has included increasing the number of trained psychiatrists and teaching field healthcare workers to identify people who are especially vulnerable. One of the biggest challenges is to prevent the relapse of people with previous mental health problems. These people were overlooked prior to the tsunami, and are likely to be forgotten in the reconstruction phase too.

Networking and collaboration

Evidence from this research suggests the focus of the disability sector is upwards towards those seen as having financial and decision-making power. This was found to be particularly true among those lobbying for accessible reconstruction after the tsunami. The researchers did not find evidence of horizontal networking with people who were affected by the tsunami but had been marginalized for reasons other than impairment.

Funding does not create inclusion

Many of the issues that arose in this research are similar to those found in other contexts. The aspect of the tsunami that is unique is the unprecedented level of funding available. Despite this, a fully accessible/inclusive environment for the whole community is not being created. This exposes the fallacy that disabled people would be included if sufficient resources were available. In Sri Lanka, a government agent reported that when funding reaches local aid workers it is allocated to specific budget lines with no consideration of disabled people's needs. Therefore, he claimed, if any extra money is spent on making accessible shelters and sanitation systems it would result in fewer being constructed. If this is the case, then it suggests that the focus of lobbying needs to be at policy making rather than implementation level.

Several international organisations argue that the disability movement has weak capacity and if the lobbying work were to be postponed until disabled people's organisations are able to take this on independently it will be too late. The buildings will be constructed without consideration of access. However, the result may be to postpone the urgent need for funding and capacity building of the disability movement.

Many international organisations spoke of their concern about public image. The unprecedented levels of public funding means evidence is needed to prove that the money has been effectively used. If not, future fundraising may become even more difficult. On the south coast of Sri Lanka, where the media readily go, the roads are lined with brightly coloured tents and the flag of the respective donor country. On the east coast, which was far more severely affected, but where the media rarely reach, people sleep under UN tarpaulins. Until disability becomes an issue of widespread public concern it is unlikely to be prioritised where public relations are crucial.

Many people from the bigger international agencies spoke of the novel problem of having so much money they do not know how to spend it. Smaller INGOs that may not have directly received public donations are being offered funding from the larger organisations. However, there appears to be more reluctance to fund local organisations, including DPOs, directly.

Training manuals and guidelines

There are now several manuals and guidelines that promote the inclusion of disability in emergencies. The most widely used is probably the Sphere handbook. It is aimed at 'improving the effectiveness and accountability of humanitarian assistance'. Much work was done to revise the 2004 edition, incorporating the inclusion of disabled people as a cross-cutting issue:.

In order to maximise the coping strategies of those affected by disasters, it is important to acknowledge the differing vulnerabilities, needs and capacities of affected groups. Specific factors, such as gender, age, disability and HIV/AIDS status, affect vulnerability and shape people's ability to cope and survive in a disaster context (Sphere 2004:45).

Whilst this is an improvement on previous editions, Sphere has been criticised for its quantitative approach and 'standardising' what are more socially embedded issues such as disability. There are several other manuals, guidelines and policies on including disabled people, for example those by ITDG, SHIA, Oxfam, DfID and the EU. The Sri Lankan government has guidelines on architectural accessibility, which were unratified at the time of the research. Little evidence was found of these resources being promoted, let alone implemented.

Other organisations offer a kind of 'tool kit' approach to inclusion, for example focusing on community-based rehabilitation (CBR), such as that published by Mobility International (Heinicke-Motsch and Sygall 2004). Some explore specific issues, such as the needs of children with disabilities, models of therapy, treatment and education, and how some of these have been applied where resources are scarce (Zinkin and Mcconachie 1995). HelpAge International (HAI) has prepared guidelines on including older people in emergency relief and many of these issues are similar for disabled people (HelpAge 2000/2001). However, equipping someone with the 'tools' to implement a disability-inclusive programme is not the same as giving disabled people equal rights. To address disability equality issues would necessitate changing power relations to ensure that disabled people actually have some control over each stage of the process, such as setting the agenda, implementation and monitoring.

Key Recommendations

Key recommendations that have come out of the research are as follows:

- *The social model.* More training and support is needed on the social model and disability rights and how they relate to data collection, research, programme planning, implementation and evaluation. This needs to be done at field level for local agencies, including DPOs and international agency field staff. The disability movement could provide training for international organisations in what the social model means in practice.

- *Inclusion in policy and practice.* More research, guidelines and training are needed to explore and overcome barriers to implementing full inclusion, as well as to investigate the impact of changes in language and rhetoric.
- *Resource materials.* Many different manuals and resources exist for emergency work: some include disability more than others. Research is needed on who is using what, or not, and why and why not? Training and awareness raising are needed at all levels to ensure manuals are known about and used.
- *Engagement with development issues.* The links between disability issues, general development issues and other issues of discrimination and exclusion need to be explored and alliances made. For example, the effect of water privatisation on disabled people needs to be examined and links made with others working on these issues. This will create a more powerful and coherent force for lobbying and more genuinely inclusive work. This requires the disability movement and aid agencies to consciously recognise and engage with the political issues.
- *Effective alliances.* The disability movement needs to make clear decisions regarding where to prioritise attention and with whom to make alliances. It should not take minor changes in rhetoric as indicators of meaningful change in itself. Similarly being invited to participate should not in itself be taken as an indicator of inclusion.
- *Lobbying.* There is a need to examine the effect on local DPOs and NGOs when INGOs lead lobbying work. More exploration is needed on how local organisations could be strengthened quickly in order to respond to an emergency. Long term funding and training is needed to build the capacity of DPOs in lobbying and campaigning work.
- *DPO representation.* The extent that DPOs represent disabled people who are affected by an emergency needs to be investigated and also how representation could be increased.
- *Programme linked research.* Although perhaps very tsunami specific, many people complained of the numbers of people coming to ask questions, without giving practical assistance. It is important to link research to action/funding/programmes and to be aware of power issues. People are likely to say what they think funders or others with power want to hear, particularly if there is a possibility of getting money.
- *Needs assessments.* There must be more analysis of who undertakes needs

assessments, in consultation with whom and how decisions over allocation of resources are made. DPOs should be involved in the planning and
conducting of needs assessments.

- *Finance.* More work is needed on what proportion of finance and resources have gone to DPOs and local organisations, and a comparison
done with situations where there is less funding available. Funding and
capacity building support is needed for the disability movement to ensure
that it is able to speak on its own behalf.

- *Development fashion and mental health.* Agencies need to respond
carefully to the current fashion for 'psychosocial' interventions and to be
aware of the on-going stigma and exclusion experienced by people with
mental illness.

- *Collaboration and networking.* More efforts need to be made by all
stakeholders to encourage horizontal alliances and grass roots consultation systems

- *Diversity.* More research is needed which takes account of the diversity of
the disabled community This should include consulting disabled people
of different ages, gender, ethnicity, class and types of impairment.

Conclusions

Overall this work was pioneering in its attempt to apply emancipatory research
principles to a large-scale disaster situation. It was hampered by the limited time
available, combined with the constraints of conducting participatory research
in an emergency situation. It was found that many of the issues facing disabled
people in a disaster situation are similar to those found in development more
generally. The most important of these is that despite rhetorical claims of inclusion and civil society involvement, the development agenda is overwhelmingly
set by powerful political and economic business interests, both internationally
and domestically, rather than by poor and marginalized people. The result is
that the rhetoric of inclusion and accessibility is used for the most part to give
credence to agendas that are deeply destructive to the poor community as a
whole, including disabled people.

There is a widespread reluctance among international NGOs to address this
question. This is reflected in the common assertion that their work is apolitical,
which in effect means avoiding addressing the causes of disabled people and
other poor peoples' subordination, inequality and exclusion.

On the more positive side, a lot of lobbying has taken place to push for accessible reconstruction after the tsunami. Also, many organisations now at least pay some attention to disability issues, whether this be in terms of having some form of guidelines or changing the language used. The challenge is to get this change reflected in genuine equality for disabled people.

Outside the disability sector, many people are organising against the top-down, business-centred approach apparent in the tsunami reconstruction agenda. The disability sector has even been invited to join. There were significant levels of organised resistance and unity among poor communities fighting for their rights within the reconstruction.

The research itself was a means of gathering and sharing information between the people involved. It helped disabled people approach some of the bigger agencies, asking for information but also pushing for inclusion. It has stimulated further discussion and research into this important area and facilitated growing awareness that many of the issues outlined here such as poverty, social exclusion and marginalisation, cannot be eradicated without seriously addressing disabled people's rights and needs.

References

Access for All website. Available at:
http://www.accessforall.lk/organisation.htm

Consortium of Humanitarian Agencies (Sri Lanka)., nd. Available at: http://www.humanitarian-srilanka.org/

Development with Disabled Network website. Available at:
http://www.itdg.org/?id=tsunami_disabled

Disability Intergroup Meeting., 2005. Tsunami – the impact on disabled persons: how to design the emergency relief and reconstruction effort to ensure inclusion and access of disabled people. Report of Meeting held at European Parliament, Strasbourg 23rd February. Available at:
http://www.edf-feph.org/apdg/minutes/FINAL%20Report%20of%20Disability%20Intergroup%20meeting%20on%20Tsunami%20Feb%202005.doc

EURODAD., 2003. Sri Lanka People's Statement on PRSP Ahead of Tokyo Donors Conference. Available at:
http://www.eurodad.org/articles/default.aspx?id=480

Government of Sri Lanka., 2002. *Regaining Sri Lanka Vision and Strategy for Accelerated Development.* World Bank Poverty Reduction Strategy Paper. Available at:
http://povlibrary.worldbank.org/files/Sri_Lanka_PRSP.pdf

Harris, A. with Enfield, S., 2003. *Disability, Equality, and Human Rights: A Training Manual for Development and Humanitarian Organisations.* Oxford: Oxfam in association with Action on Disability and Development.

HelpAge International., 2000. Emergencies: Background: Guidelines for best Practice. London: HelpAge International. Available at:
http://www.helpage.org/emergencies/emergBPG/emergBPG.html

HelpAge International., 2001. Emergencies and aging: A Position Paper. London: HelpAge International. Available at:
http://www.helpage.org/images/pdfs/briefing%20papers/EmergenciesandAgeing.PDF

HelpAge International with UNHCR., nd. Older People in Disasters and Humanitarian Emergencies: Guidelines for Best Practice. London: HelpAge International.
http://www.helpage.org/images/pdfs/bpg.pdf

Heinicke-Motsch, K. and Sygall, S.O., 2004. Building An Inclusive Development Community: A Manual on Including People with Disabilities in International Development Programs. Mobility International USA.

ITDG., 2004. Reconstruction Process– Guidelines for Planning in the Rebuilding Process – Resource Pack. Available at:
http://www.itdg.org/docs/region_south_asia/guidelines-planning-rebuilding.pdf

ITDG., 2005. Inclusion of Persons with Disabilities into Tsunami. Available at:
http://www.itdg.org/docs/region_south_asia/tsunami-reconstruction-disability.pdf

International Disability and Development Consortium (IDDC)., 2000. Disability and Conflict: Report of an IDDC Seminar (Draft). Available at:
http://www.iddc.org.uk/dis_dev/key_issues/dis_confl_rep.doc

Jones, H., 2005. *Designing water & sanitation for disabled people and other vulnerable groups*. Loughborough University Water, Engineering and Development Centre (WEDC). Available at:
http://wedc.lboro.ac.uk/projects/new_projects3.php?id=60

Klein, N., 2005., The Rise of Disaster Capitalism. ZNET. Available at:
http://www.zmag.org/content/showarticle.cfm?SectionID=13&ItemID=7680

Ministry of Social Welfare., 2003. Social Research Study on Disability. Colombo: Government of Sri Lanka.

MONLAR., 2005. Sri Lankan Government using tsunami to privatize water. 25th February. Available at:
www.geocities.com/monlarslk

Reality of Aid. Website. Available at:
http://www.realityofaid.org/rchecknews.php?table=rc_jun05&id=1

Reliefweb, Website. Available at:
http://www.reliefweb.int/rw/dbc.nsf/doc108?OpenForm&emid=TS-2004-000147-LKA&rc=3#show

Sri Lanka Development Forum., 2005. Civil Society Statement. Available at:
http://www.geocities.com/monlardocuments/documents/tsunami/sl_devt_forum_cs_statement.doc

TAFREN., 2005. Rebuilding the tsunami affected area. Implementation plan. Available at :
http://www.tafren.gov.lk/terms-of-reference.php

Venkatesh, B., 2004. Community Based Rehabilitation (CBR) in a Globalising Environment. Paper Presented on Poverty and Disability at the WHO Consultation to Develop Guidelines on CBR, Geneva.

WHO., nd. Suicide Rates (per 100,000), by country, year, and gender. Available at:
http://www.who.int/mental_health/prevention/suicide/suiciderates/en/

Zinkin , Pam and Mcconachie, Helen., 1995. *Disabled children and developing countries*. London: MacKeith Press.

CHAPTER 13

Improving participatory appraisal approaches with rural disabled people: A pilot project in Pursat province, Cambodia

Steve Harknett

This study examined the participation of disabled people in the planning stage of community development projects. Disabled people's inclusion is of concern in all stages of the development process, but particularly so in planning, as lack of participation early in the development process can lead to institutionalised exclusion of disabled people later, for example, in programme design and implementation.

The study piloted ways in which inexperienced, rural disabled people could learn and use participatory rural appraisal (PRA) methods and how participation of rural disabled people in village PRA exercises could be increased. The focus of the research was on the processes of the PRA (the performance of the PRA team and the participation of disabled villagers in the fieldwork) rather than its outputs, such as the results of the PRA exercises.

This research was the first study of disabled people's participation in development processes in Cambodia, a country where disabled people experience widespread social exclusion. It has wider significance because, although in other parts of the developing world, notably sub-Saharan Africa, disabled people's voices are heard much more loudly in development debates, it is usually only the voices of an urban educated elite of disabled people. This research involved uneducated, village-level disabled people with no previous experience in development work.

Disabled people's participation

Disabled people in developing countries tend to be excluded from development initiatives for many reasons. They are often the poorest, most uneducated people in society and are marginalised because of poverty and discrimination. This exclusion, coupled with physical difficulties in mobility that many face, lead to them being relatively invisible in society. Also, disabled people do not usually live together in one place but are scattered throughout a community, so they rarely have opportunities to come together to raise their profile. Even when disabled people are brought into the development debate, difficulties in communication and understanding - for people who are deaf, blind or have learning difficulties - present barriers to participation. Also, disabled people who have suffered a lifetime of exclusion often have had little experience in being asked their opinion, and their input into development planning may therefore be of limited value. This can reinforce development practitioners' attitudes that disabled people cannot effectively participate and the belief that they need non-disabled 'experts' to make decisions for them. Such barriers to participation are particularly serious for disabled women and children and people with severe or multiple impairments.

Disabled people's invisibility is particularly acute in Cambodia. Unlike in many developing countries, the Cambodian disability sector is still dominated by organisations for rather than of disabled people. The national disability rights movement is in its infancy – a national disabled people's organisation (Cambodian Disabled People's Organisation) exists but it has very weak grassroots support. No disability legislation has ever been passed in Cambodia. Cultural Cambodian beliefs about disability are rooted in the charitable paradigm, with disabled people seen as passive receivers of aid. There is little awareness of the concept of empowerment of disabled people. Cambodian society also has a strong sense of hierarchy and marked social division between those who have power and influence - the rich and those who provide such as NGOs and those who don't - the poor, and those who receive. Such beliefs persist among many NGOs, whose staff may view disabled people as 'objects' of projects rather than active participants, and they plan and design disability programmes accordingly, with little input from disabled people themselves.

To try to bring marginalised people, including disabled people, into development processes, development practitioners use participatory methods such as PRA. PRA reverses the traditional roles of the external researcher and the community being researched. The researcher 'hands over the stick', allowing communities to study and analyse issues themselves, draw conclusions and make recommendations about their priorities and how to solve their problems. The community manages and owns this process and presents the results to the external researcher (e.g. a development agency). The community uses simple, accessible methods and approaches they can understand without the need for external experts. The development agency's role is to be 'on tap not on top'. That is, being available to assist where necessary, but not in control.

This shift involves a complete reversal of power relations between the development agency and the community and a corresponding change in attitudes. In practice, however, many exercises which claim to be participatory fall short of the ideal. While they often use PRA tools (mapping, ranking, etc.), control and ownership of the process is maintained by the development agency. Power relations between the development agency and the community have not changed. This is often reinforced in PRA training programmes, which often put more emphasis on techniques and tools and less on development workers' relations with the community. In Cambodia, and no doubt in other countries, development workers often pay large sums of money to study PRA in prestigious schools in the capital Phnom Penh. The effect of this is to mystify PRA, distancing development 'experts' from communities still further and widening the power gap between them rather than narrowing it.

DDSP and participation

Disability Development Services Pursat (DDSP) is a Cambodian NGO in Pursat province, a poor rural province about 185 km northwest of the capital Phnom Penh. The west of the province is still heavily contaminated by landmines remaining from Cambodia's years of conflict. DDSP was established in 2003 and works with disabled people, their families and their communities, in areas such as community-based rehabilitation (CBR), inclusive education and rehabilitation of people with spinal cord injury and cerebral palsy.

DDSP has worked to narrow the power-gap between its staff and its target population. Unlike many NGOs in Cambodia, DDSP fieldworkers regularly stay overnight in villages, often sleeping in the homes of disabled people, in order to build close relationships with the communities they serve. DDSP has regularly carried out PRAs to gain a deeper understanding of the communities' needs (DDSP 2003). However the organisation also recognised that the level of participation of disabled people in its needs assessments and project planning was inadequate. DDSP's PRAs were designed and implemented by staff and local government officials. Bringing local government officials into the PRA process was a step in the right direction towards increasing community participation; however, disabled people were still marginalised. They were consulted but did not play any meaningful role in planning and implementing the survey or making recommendations.

Recognising that it had to do more to increase disabled people's participation, DDSP designed this pilot research project to move disabled people to the very centre of DDSP's work. The project piloted PRA methods and approaches which were controlled by disabled people themselves. The project took place in February 2005 supported by the DFID Disability KaR Programme. It was hoped that the study would build disabled people's capacity in community development skills, challenge community attitudes towards disabled people and change attitudes and work practice within DDSP.

The main objective of the research project was to review and improve the practice of PRA with and by disabled people. It looked at disabled people's participation in all stages of the PRA from the beginning to the end of the process. The research sought to address questions in three main areas:

How best can inexperienced, uneducated disabled people be trained in PRA?

What PRA tools are the most appropriate, i.e. can be easily used and understood by the disabled facilitators and the villagers alike?

What are the barriers to disabled people's participation in village PRA exercises and how can they be overcome?

Methodology

A PRA team of seven people was formed, including five disabled people and two non-disabled people (DDSP staff). The five disabled people, three men and two women, all came from rural areas. The three men were small-scale farmers and the two women did domestic work at home. One of the five had never been to school while three had been to primary school but not completed it. One had started at secondary school but not completed it. Three of the five were completely or partly illiterate. Four of the five had conditions affecting their mobility and one had a learning difficulty.

The research had five stages:

1. Training in PRA – a three-day workshop was held for the PRA team which included learning about the purpose of the PRA, and tools and approaches. The team designed the PRA exercises, including deciding research areas to be addressed, tools to be used and a time-frame. An external facilitator with experience in PRA and community development led this workshop.

2. Fieldwork – the team carried out PRA exercises in three villages (Prohoas Kbal, Prey Veang and Prey O Mal) for three or four days per village.

The three villages were all remote and poor. Two of them were in areas formerly affected by landmines – one is still being demined. In all the PRA activities, the disabled team members were encouraged to play as large a role as possible, with the two DDSP staff in a supporting role. Fieldwork, based on research topics decided in the workshop, included community identification of disabled people, role plays on community attitudes to disabled people, disabled people's problems and priorities for action, income generating activities, disabled children's education, comparative wealth (disabled and non-disabled people), life-lines and time-lines, service-mapping and village presentations.

3. Monitoring and evaluation – the PRA team had feedback sessions at the end of each day to discuss problems. A final evaluation was carried out at the end of the whole exercise.

4. Analysis and presentation of the results – both at village level (to get feedback from villagers) and in Pursat at DDSP's office, in order to make recommendations to DDSP on future strategy in the three villages.

5. Visits to other NGOs – the PRA team visited Landmine Disability Support (LMDS) in Kampong Chhnang province and Handicap International Belgium (the Capacity Building of People with Disability in the Community (CABDIC) programme) in Banteay Meanchey province, to learn about their PRA practice in community work with disabled people.

Findings

The main focus of the research project was on the processes rather than the outputs. Although the outputs, covering the research topics described above, were useful and contributed to DDSP planning in the three villages, this chapter will focus on the lessons learned in the process of carrying out the PRAs.

Training inexperienced disabled people in participatory methods

The three-day PRA workshop helped the participants to understand the purpose of the PRA, make decisions about what topics would be studied and what methods would be used. The team understood the importance of having all disabled people participate. Factors which contributed to the success of the training workshop were:

Focus on confidence building. The very term 'training' can be threatening to uneducated people who imagine it as formal learning using literacy skills which they don't have. The training was termed a 'meeting' and other alien terminology such as PRA was avoided. Steps taken to build participants' confidence were:

Keeping the training group small to reduce shyness

Starting the training with a simple, fun activity, 'picture introductions' (participants drawing pictures of themselves and their home and using them to talk about their lives), so they could experience success early in the training.

Being realistic in what the participants could learn. PRA tools needing advanced literacy, group facilitation or presentation skills were avoided.

Creating a comfortable environment. Participants and facilitators sat on the floor in the traditional Cambodian way without tables or chairs. The training took place in a quiet, private house rather than an office. Icebreakers, humour and team-building exercises built relationships between participants.

The facilitator was aware of the participants' educational level and used appropriate communication methods. No written documents were used, only verbal or pictorial methods. The facilitator used frequent reviews and repetition of key points, and he proceeded at the pace of the participants' learning. Periods of study and concentration were balanced with breaktimes, music and games for relaxation.

Considering physical accessibility in the training venue and accommodation (access to buildings, traveling distances, road conditions, latrines, etc.) and personal needs - for example the woman with learning difficulties acted as an excellent personal assistant to the woman wheelchair-user for things such as toileting and bathing.

Not assuming that the disabled people automatically had solidarity with other disabled people or had comprehensive knowledge of all types of impairment. The training included understanding of the nine types of impairment and respect for and understanding of all disabled people. Emphasis was put on including marginalised groups such as people with visual, hearing and learning difficulties, people with mental health problems, disabled women, disabled children and elderly people. Overcoming barriers to participation such as distance, shyness and dealing with dominant people were also discussed.

Including participatory monitoring of the training throughout and acting on any problems/ideas that participants raised.

For such a novel workshop, difficulties were bound to arise. They included:

Facilitator preparation – the facilitator was an experienced PRA facilitator, but it was the first time he had trained people of such a low educational level, which is perhaps indicative of the elitism of development in Cambodia. He quickly realised that his written hand-outs were useless as most of the participants could not read them! Although the facilitator was flexible and responsive to the participants' needs, he could have benefited from more prior preparation.

Duration – the workshop was held in Pursat town because the disabled people came from several different villages. However this was far from their homes and it was difficult for some of them to stay away from home for so long. It was also difficult for them to concentrate on the topic for so long even when activities were interspersed with recreation activities and games. Ideally the workshop should have been held nearer to participants' homes and structured differently, perhaps with half-day sessions over a longer period of time.

Need for differential training goals – in any workshop participants have different levels of understanding, but this was particularly so in this workshop where one participant had learning difficulties. Rather than expecting her to reach the same learning goals as the other participants, which led to time loss and frustration, it would have been more realistic to have set different goals for her which were appropriate to her ability but which were still useful to the PRA.

Appropriate PRA tools

The disabled team-members used some tools successfully but had difficulty with others. The tools they found easiest to use were those based on various pictorial methods. However, although it is commonplace for community workers to use pictures rather than words to communicate with villagers, it is often forgotten that these pictures are usually drawn by people outside the community. People from within the community who are illiterate generally do not have experience in drawing, so the PRA team needed to practise this. Poorly-drawn pictures can be as unintelligible to illiterate people as text. Bearing this in mind, the methods used included the following:

- an illustrated household wealth surveying tool was developed and used to compare the wealth (measured by ownership of cows, pigs, TV, etc.) of households with a disabled person and without a disabled person;
- pictures of different types of impairment, copied on large cards from key CBR texts like David Werner's Disabled Village Children. (1987) These were used to raise awareness about the nine types of impairment and identify disabled people in the village;
- pictorial presentations - illustrated graphs showing prevalence of types of impairment;
- activities directly and concretely related to their daily lives, e.g. their income generating activities, daily routines and the services they use. For example;
- ranking disabled people's income-generating activities. The results were used to discuss the difficulties they had with certain income-generating activities, why some activities were more important than others, why they were not doing certain activities, and what activities they are not doing but would like to do;
- daily activities – drawing daily activity calendars to depict the disabled person's routine from getting up in the morning to going to bed at night. These were used to highlight livelihood activities; and
- service mapping – drawing diagrams to depict all the services (governmental and non-governmental) in the village, showing which were most important to disabled people (near the centre of the diagram) and which were least important (far from the centre). The diagrams were used to identify gaps where disabled people thought there were few or no services.

The use of other PRA tools proved less successful, for several reasons. With more time for training, some of these problems could have been addressed, while others were more deep-rooted.

The reasons for lack of success were:

- low educational level – the disabled facilitators had difficulty in PRA activities involving literacy and numeracy skills, e.g. using written questionnaires and calculating percentages from wealth-ranking data;
- lack of community development experience – the PRA workshop did not cover community development skills and did not address the disabled

facilitators' attitudes about empowerment and self-help. Consequently they shared the same mind-set as other villagers. For example, in the PRA exercise about developing solutions to disabled people's problems, villagers responded with a list of things they wanted NGOs to give them. Facilitation was needed to get the villagers to think of ways in which the community can help themselves. The disabled facilitators, not having had training on self-help, were unable to do this; and

- lack of confidence – many of the disabled PRA team-members, especially the women, had low self-esteem because of their impairment, experience of social exclusion and low educational level, and had difficulty using PRA tools which involved activities in public, especially performing role-plays. Some of the team also felt uncomfortable talking to people in authority, e.g. teachers and village chiefs. The women in the PRA team in particular had difficulty asking questions to male figures of authority.

Enabling all disabled people participate

In the field, the team was constantly reminded to try to include all disabled people in the village in PRA activities and to overcome barriers to their participation. 'All' meant disabled men and women (including elderly people), boys and girls. It also included people with all types of impairments, including those with severe impairments or people with hidden or misunderstood conditions such as deafness or mental health problems. Another category was location. This meant people living in the centre of the village and people living in the forest where there were no roads. 'Participation' required knowing about the PRA activity, being able to physically attend the meeting and being able to join in actively. This involved the team being proactive, attentive and ready to provide additional, individual support where necessary. Of course one cannot coerce disabled people into participating in a PRA meeting. They have the freedom to choose not to participate and they may have good reasons for making this decision. However, the team sought ways to address obstacles to participation in these three areas. Examples of good practice are set out below:

Ensuring disabled people know about the PRA activity

In identifying disabled people to invite to the PRA meeting, the team did not rely too much on local leaders' (village chiefs or others in leadership positions) knowledge of the disabled people in the village. A village can cover a large area and chiefs' knowledge is often incomplete, both about the geographical area of the village and the scope of the term 'disability'. In one village, the chief reported that there were no disabled children in his village, but the PRA team came across a boy with learning difficulties wandering in the road outside the chief's house.

The PRA team disseminated information about PRA meetings at the sub-village level, either via krom-leaders (krom are smaller administrative units under the village leader) or by house-to-house visiting.

Sometimes a disabled person was absent from a PRA meeting and other villagers offered a reason, e.g. due to sickness or being busy with income-generating activities. In such cases the PRA team checked at the person's home because in some cases their absence was actually due to not receiving the information about the meeting, or having a problem in attending which the PRA team could help with. In other cases, villagers may have even had reasons to deliberately try to exclude him/her.

Ensuring physical attendance

The PRA team used several small motorbikes in the villages which enabled the team to respond to individual difficulties disabled people had in physically travelling to the meeting, even from inaccessible parts of the village. In one village the village chief said he had heard of a man with severe mobility difficulties living far away, but had never met him. The team set off on a long search to find him and eventually tracked him down living in a remote forested area. He was unable to walk so the team brought him to a meeting by motorbike. Many villagers were surprised as they had never seen him before.

In another village a severely disabled orphan was living with his aunt and uncle who neglected him because he was not their own child. The aunt and uncle were not interested in coming to the PRA meeting so they needed additional encouragement and help with transport.

In some cases the disabled person did not come to the PRA meeting but sent a family member to represent him/her, such as a spouse or a child. While there were sometimes good reasons for this, the team would make a home visit to explore these reasons and encourage him/her to join in the next meeting. The PRA team did not want to reinforce the traditional practice of disabled people remaining hidden at home and relying on family members to represent them.

Encouraging active joining in

During PRA meetings, team-members were attentive to processes and interactions. Rather than sitting all together at the front, the team-members spread out and sat among the participants to observe if anyone was having difficulties understanding or participating. They provided additional encouragement or explanation if needed:

- several ways were used to help people with hearing impairment. Sometimes the team sought family assistance – there is no formal sign language in rural Cambodia but family members can often communicate with gestures. People with hearing problems were also invited to sit at the front of meetings so they could hear more easily or could lip-read. A team-member sat near people with hearing problems to provide additional explanation.
- meeting facilitators used simple language and repeated instructions to ensure that people with learning difficulties or hearing difficulties had understood. The facilitator asked questions to check participants' understanding;
- written exercises were kept to a minimum because of illiteracy, but where written flipcharts were used, short key-points were written using large, clear letters and they were accompanied with clear verbal explanations; and
- facilitators were aware of domination in meetings by certain individuals. Although disabled people are generally marginalised in the community, some have rank and influence and can stifle other people's expression.

Other NGOs' experience
The research project visited the community disability programmes of LMDS and CABDIC to learn from their experience in using PRA with disabled people. These visits found that despite claims that PRA was being used and PRA training having been given to staff, methods and approaches were still being used which did not allow for sufficient participation from villagers and more importantly the target group, disabled people. This was manifested in problems such as:

- dominance by NGO staff and local government officials, which stifled the ability for ordinary villagers to express problems and solutions themselves. Care and affirmative action was needed to remove strong influences from others (LMDS 2004?). LMDS felt that this experience of PRA was typical in Cambodia, where a tendency for 'social superiors who know best' is deep-seated and a cultural characteristic (J. Lowrie, pers. comm.);

- evidence that in decision making the NGO was on top, not the villagers. Such things as the timing of PRA activities being planned without considering villagers' farming and household commitments;
- in CABDIC's PRAs, there were no village meetings to get feedback from or have dialogue with the community at the end of the exercise. Data was taken away for analysis by CABDIC staff. LMDS did use group work in their PRAs, but there was a lack of participatory facilitation skills and methods, such as using ice-breakers, story-telling, and group-building exercises. (LMDS 2004?); and
- insufficient use of PRA data to shape the project's plans. LMDS did use PRA to input directly into project strategy. In CABDIC, however, the PRAs simply identified disabled people who could participate in pre-determined project activities rather than soliciting ideas from the disabled people as to what the project activities should be. Such a lack of using PRA data indicates a failure of the NGO to listen in any meaningful way to its target group and to value their opinions. These are the kind of actions which render the whole PRA exercise a waste of time and can lead to community disillusionment.

These problems suggested that PRA training was not addressing underlying attitudes and the power dynamics between NGO workers and their target groups. LMDS noted the difficulty in finding a PRA trainer with a genuinely participatory attitude, reflecting the state of PRA training in Cambodia. According to the LMDS Director, improving PRA practice is 'all about changing attitudes, not just in token or tacit gestures, but in real change towards inculcating true respect for the opinions of other people' (J. Lowrie, pers. comm.).

Conclusions: lessons learned
Promoting disabled people's participation through PRA benefits disabled people, their communities and development organisations. In this study, the disabled team-members gained skills and experience in community assessment, and their confidence and competence in carrying out PRA exercises increased. Communities could see that disabled people could play an important role in community development. The family of the woman with learning difficulties, who they considered quite useless, were surprised that DDSP was interested in bringing her out of their village to the provincial town for a workshop and giving her work. The presence of a paraplegic woman sent a powerful awareness-rais-

ing message to communities – she attracted a lot of stares as most villagers had never seen a woman in a wheelchair before.

For development organisations, truly effective community development with disabled people can only be realised through promoting disabled people's participation at grass-roots level. This research has indicated some ways in which disabled people, even when they are illiterate and inexperienced, can play this role. It also showed the need to bring disabled women and people with learning difficulties into the development process, given that they often face particular discrimination. Issues that need to be addressed to increase disabled people's participation are:

Training in PRA – the training should focus on confidence building and community development concepts like self-help and participation, should be as relaxed and non-technical as possible, and be adaptable to the speed of the participants. It should include disability awareness. Facilitators should be well-prepared and should have experience working with people who are illiterate. The training is a long-term process and should address deeper needs such as low self-esteem and illiteracy.

Use of appropriate tools – the inexperienced disabled facilitators in this research performed best with PRA tools related directly and concretely to their lives, and tools using pictures. As facilitators become more experienced, so the range of PRA tools they could handle could increase.

Maximising village level participation – PRA fieldwork should take steps to ensure that all disabled people in the village know about the PRA exercise, that they can physically attend the meeting, and they actively join in the meeting. This often involves paying extra attention and making special effort to individual disabled people's situations and problems.

NGO staff's attitudes and practices – in the short term, this study helped to change DDSP staff's attitudes – it was the first time for DDSP staff to work alongside the organisation's beneficiaries and it challenged the traditional NGO-client relationship. However further PRAs carried out in January 2006, when DDSP extended into new villages, showed that the longer-term impact has been mixed – some lessons had sunk in and were applied while others had been forgotten. Disabled people were included in the PRA team, but not in the majority of the teams. Some PRA methods and analysis were used which were understood only by the better-educated staff-members and not by the disabled people. In some instances, disabled people's participation had been reduced to tokenism, for example reading out flipcharts prepared by staff without understanding what they meant. This showed that the change in attitudes and practice among DDSP staff is a journey and needs continual reinforcement and prompts to realise a transformation in relationships between NGOs and the communities they serve. PRA training and supervision offered by development training institutions and NGOs to their staff should address attitudes and power dynamics, rather than teaching the tools and techniques.

References

Disability Development Services., Pursat 2003. Disabled people and their communities: a Participatory Rural Appraisal of Prohal, Chong Rok and O Thkov villages, Pursat Province. DDSP.

LMDS., 2004. Landmine Disability Support Quarterly Report to 31 December 2003.

LMDS., 2004?. PRA Module.

Werner, D., 1987. Disabled Village Children. Hesperian Foundation

Situational analysis and assessment of education for disabled children in Bangladesh, South Asia, East Asia and South Africa

Rabiul Hasan

Whilst the right to education for all children/people is acknowledged in the Universal Declaration of Human Rights, varied educational systems have been established to meet the needs of disabled children. The most familiar of these is 'special education', in which disabled children are educated separately from their non-disabled counterparts. The last decade has seen a move towards a more inclusive and integrated approach in which disabled children are educated alongside non-disabled children, usually in mainstream schools. All these systems appear to be universal, with many countries adopting a segregated (i.e. special education) approach and latterly, moving towards a more inclusive approach – with varying success.

The research in this area looked specifically at the major shortfalls in the design and implementation of special and inclusive/integrated education processes for disabled children. In addition it explored the merits of each system in terms of the advantages offered to disabled children, particularly in relation to the impact of enrolment, repetition, dropout and attitude towards different systems. The countries covered were Bangladesh, Nepal, Vietnam and South Africa.

Background

All children have a right to education. The Universal Declaration of Human Rights (1948) declares 'Everyone has the right to education; (and) education shall be directed to the full development of the human personality and to the strengthening of respect for human rights and fundamental freedoms'. Despite this, in the Asian and Pacific region less than 10% of disabled children and young people have access to any form of education, compared to an enrolment rate of over 70% for non-disabled children and young people in primary education.

Meeting the educational needs of disabled children has historically involved establishing educational settings specifically for disabled children, including for specific impairments, that were separate from mainstream educational establishments. Known widely as special education, this system serves to separate disabled children from their non-disabled peers. Since the Universal Declaration, the disadvantages of the special education system have been debated, in terms of the effect of 'removing' disabled children from not only mainstream school, but mainstream life activities, and the repercussions of this on enabling them as children, and subsequently as adults, to be accepted as important and valued citizens in society. The concept of disability as a social issue, rather than a medical issue, has also become more understood and prompted a change in attitude towards a more integrated, and latterly, inclusive system.

The move away from segregated educational establishments to those which integrated the education of children with varied needs was addressed directly by UNESCO a decade ago (1996). Integrated education involves the admission of children with special educational needs into mainstream schools – i.e., 'integrating' them into an existing system – changes are required of learners so that they can 'fit in' to an already established system. Extra support is provided where necessary.

Taking this concept a step further, the World Conference on Special Needs Education in Salamanca, Spain, in 1994, adopted the principle of inclusive education in which differences among learners is recognised and the system itself is adapted to accommodate the needs of children. The focus here is on overcoming the barriers that prevent the full range of learning needs being met, through adapting the whole curriculum to include issues pertinent to the needs of specific children (as opposed to teaching being provided in separate classrooms, in mainstream schools). The value of inclusive education was restated at the World Education Forum in Senegal in 2000.

All countries adopt differing educational systems for disabled children, and this research explores why particular systems are pursued and what the challenges associated with them are. Exploring this is key, given that disabled children are least likely to challenge the educational system and are the most poorly educated in developing countries. They are also more likely than non-disabled children to suffer from lack of education, specifically due to their impairment, not necessarily because of their ability to learn. In addition there is a plethora of international commitments, national policies and legislation with regard to educating disabled children, not least the Millennium Development Goals (MDGs). Although disabled children are not mentioned specifically, Goal

2 aims to 'achieve universal primary education' and to do this by 'ensuring that by 2015 children everywhere, boys and girls alike, will be able to complete a full course of primary schooling'. Goal 3 aims to 'promote gender equity and empower women' with a target to 'eliminate gender disparity in primary and secondary education, preferably by 2005 and at all levels of education no later than 2015'. Researching the reasons why/how educational systems are meeting the needs of, or failing, disabled children is therefore important.

Educational systems in the following countries were reviewed: South Africa; Vietnam; Nepal and Bangladesh. The countries were identified on the basis of geographical range, and differing political governance.

The objectives of the research were as follows:

- assess and analyse the shortfalls in the existing design and implementation process of education programmes for disabled children;
- assess the effectiveness and impact of existing inclusive education programmes in terms of attitude, enrolment, repetition and dropout;
- assess the impact of special versus inclusive/integrated education;
- identify successful case studies/examples from all countries on inclusion of disabled children and young people into the education system; and
- identify areas/issues and possible interventions for strengthening and promoting inclusive education, including North-South cooperation and collaboration.

Methodology
The nature and approach of the research was participatory, with two of the four research team members being disabled people. An 8-member children's consultative committee was formed to ensure the participation of disabled children in the process. Disabled Peoples Organisations (DPOs) and disabled people were also involved in the research.

Respondents were selected on the basis of information required to meet the objectives of the research. The research team ensured that children with a range of impairments were interviewed, along with an equal gender balance. Focus group discussions were held with DPOs, disabled children and parents groups. Interviews and individual interactions were held with government level personnel in the relevant ministerial department of each country; national coordinating organisations on disability issues; university departments of special education;

principals, head teachers and teachers in special, integrated and inclusive schools and senior level officials in NGOs and donor organisations.

Policy reviews and web-based literature searches and email questionnaires with the different stakeholders were carried out, along with site visits to special, integrated and inclusive schools (drawing on observation and discussion) and collecting case studies on the inclusion of disabled children and young people in educational systems.

In terms of limitations, fitting the research into only thirteen weeks was a key factor, as were the organisational details of securing visas etc to travel to Vietnam and South Africa, which meant that time in those countries was reduced. Contact with stakeholders proved difficult in Vietnam, where the contact organisation couldn't organise a focus group discussion with the parents of disabled children at the inclusive school. It also proved impossible to travel outside the city centres of Vietnam and South Africa due to time constraints, and in Nepal due to the political/security situation.

In terms of observation of each educational system in all four countries, this was not possible. Therefore special education was observed in each country, inclusive education was observed in Bangladesh and Vietnam and integrated education observed in Bangladesh only. Despite this, the educational policies of each country were researched.

The main findings

All three educational systems are practised to some degree in each country in which the research was undertaken, with special education being the initial approach to educating disabled children, followed by integrated and then inclusive education services (albeit on a limited basis). The research found that in Nepal most parents of disabled children felt they should study in special schools; South African parents preferred inclusive education and parents in Vietnam and Bangladesh did not come out strongly with an educational preference. Respondents in all countries identified common issues within each educational system that provided challenges in terms of implementation. A brief description of the provision in each country is given below, followed by a collated summary of the challenges faced by respondents in all four countries and in each system.

Bangladesh

Special, integrated and inclusive educational systems are being employed in

Bangladesh. The government Department of Social Services (DSS) manages the special and integrated schools, of which there are five special schools for blind children, seven for deaf children and one for children with learning difficulties. There are 13 special schools in all, which accommodate a total of 910 disabled children. The DSS also manages 64 integrated schools for blind children, in 64 districts, catering for the needs of 610 disabled children in total. NGOs manage many special and inclusive schools throughout Bangladesh and although there is unreliable data on exactly how many of these schools there are, it is estimated that approximately 20,000 disabled children are registered in NGO-managed schools practising special and inclusive education.

Nepal

Nepal's government and/or NGO sector operates special and integrated schools, but no inclusive schools. The government's Basic Primary Education Project supports 320 resource classes in primary schools throughout the country. The aim is for the children attending these classes to be integrated into the school to which the resource classes are attached, thereby providing an integrated system. However, the research showed that this is not happening in practise, so in fact the resource classes are providing special education. In terms of enrolment, figures from 2003 reveal that a total of 4,795 disabled children are enrolled in either government or NGO run special schools.

Vietnam

Special and inclusive education is practised in Vietnam. The government operates 82 special schools which it is converting to inclusive schools, whilst the NGO sector operates 20 special schools. There are over 1million disabled children under 15 years old in Vietnam, of whom only 10% are enrolled in education.

South Africa

Special education is the main educational provision for disabled children in South Africa, with 368 special education schools throughout the country. The government has initiated pilot projects on inclusive education, with a view to shifting all educational provision for disabled children to inclusive education.

The existing special schools enrol a total of 64,603 children – accounting for approximately 0.52% of all disabled learners in special educational settings. The national figure for disabled people of all ages is 6.55%.

Collated summary of challenges in each educational system

Special Education

The special education system is expensive and respondents in all countries noted that the number of institutions is inadequate given the level of need. Government funding is poor and sufficiently skilled resource teachers are limited as a result of inadequate training facilities, poor salaries, lack of teacher benefits and little opportunity to develop skills (such as sign language and Braille training). Special education institutions do not have an adequate supply of resources such as Braille books or equipment. In terms of the impact of the education given, there is an emphasis in special education on vocational skills training rather than formal teaching/learning. In South Africa, for example, a focus group discussion with pupils of one special school for children with epilepsy and children with learning difficulties, revealed that the children would like to participate less in vocational skills training and more in academic sessions. In addition, teaching is mostly at primary level, with only some secondary level teaching. By their very nature, special education systems serve to isolate disabled children from their non-disabled peers and society as a whole.

Integrated Education

The major challenges faced with this system are similar to those for special education, in terms of poor funding support for the schools and poor resources and support, both financially and in terms of skills development, for teachers. Only blind children are involved in integrated education in Bangladesh. Respondents felt that a positive impact of integrated education was that children are socialised with other children and it offers some children the chance to participate in a mainstream curriculum – with the potential opportunity to participate in higher mainstream education. Integrated education is less expensive than special education.

Inclusive Education

Inclusive education systems are not being widely practiced. The inclusive schools visited in Bangladesh are run by NGOs outside the formal education system. The result of this is that children with particular impairments, such as physical ones, and only a limited numbers of these children, are enrolled in inclusive schools. Furthermore, this is predominantly at pre-school level. Teachers are not adequately qualified or trained and classrooms and premises are not accessible or suitable for accommodating different disabled children with varied impairments. In Vietnam all government Special Schools are now Inclusive Schools, but they face the same issues in terms of poor financial and practical resources, lack of adequately trained teachers and physical inaccessibility. Nepal is engaged with international donors in a pilot project on inclusive education (including a teacher training course) but this is very small. In South Africa a comprehensive plan is in place for implementing inclusive education, but it is still at the pilot-project stage.

In terms of enrolment of disabled children in inclusive schools (observed in 10 inclusive schools in Bangladesh [total 2300 pupils] and 1 in Vietnam) the researchers found that in Bangladesh enrolment was 8.04% compared to 0.84% in formal schools and 22.61% in non-formal schools. The high figure for non-formal schools is related to NGOs running these schools and/or 'disability programmes' and actively enrolling disabled children. Families are motivated and encouraged (by the NGO) to enrol their children, and all services, including educational materials, are provided free of charge. In Vietnam 10% of children in the inclusive school observed were disabled (all visually impaired). The dropout rate for disabled children in inclusive schools in Bangladesh is 1.2%, with repetition (children who do not move up a class each year, but are retained in the same class for 2-3 years) 2%. In Vietnam the inclusive school observed did not report any dropout, and if a child does not secure the marks required to move up a class the school adds the necessary marks to ensure children do not repeat classes. In terms of attitudes towards disabled children, the Bangladesh respondents report that 35% of peer learners and 13% of teacher attitudes are unfriendly towards disabled children in the school.

In terms of specific impairments, observations in the Bangladeshi inclusive school system revealed that the enrolment rate of physically disabled children is highest in inclusive schools and lowest amongst children with speech and hearing difficulties. Whilst the prevalence of particular impairments in an area will have a bearing on the number of disabled children enrolled, school authorities and parent groups also claim that this situation reflects the difficulty these children have in communicating effectively. Parents groups say that the children themselves do not feel comfortable in the school environment. However the research shows that teachers are not adequately trained in supporting children with communication difficulties, a reason which is likely to contribute to such children not be enrolled in school. Physically disabled children face accessibility barriers (which in themselves are often difficult to surmount) but once in school they can participate in the mainstream curriculum and possibly do not need specialist support. The challenge posed by these children to the school is, therefore, relatively minimal.

Discussions with respondents revealed that the shortfalls identified above are seen to be the result of lack of political will to implement government educational policy. This is hampered by poor coordination and cooperation amongst ministerial departments and poor communication between professionals responsible for implementing policy. A key factor was also a socially ingrained negative attitude towards disability issues – both at political and societal levels. In many cases parents of disabled children also show lack of awareness of the educational needs of their children. In addition, South Africa has faced (and continues to face) the issue of racial prejudice. Nepal's geographical terrain is a barrier to disabled children even being able to travel to school. Respondents also identified the following important issues preventing adequate commitment to, and resourcing of, education for disabled children:

- there is a lack of reliable data on the prevalence of impairments and the needs of disabled children – data is key in terms of the bedrock on which to develop appropriate policies and implementation plans;
- educating disabled children is perceived to be a 'welfare' issue rather than a human rights or development issue. That is, the children need to be 'looked after' rather than provided with skills to enable them to earn a living, think independently etc. An example of this in Bangladesh is that overseeing the education of disabled children lies within the Ministry of Social Welfare;
- poverty contributes to an inability/lack of motivation to address the needs

of disabled children, who are seen to be a drain on resources, non-contributors to family income and support and with little part to play in society as a whole; and

- there is little knowledge amongst parents of disabled children, school management committees and/or school governing bodies about international conventions/ statements on educating disabled children, or about national policies on education. Teachers learn about these during their training, so they are aware of them, but given that morale and motivation amongst them is low it is not likely they will lobby or raise awareness of these issues.

Policy issues

All four countries' national legislation regarding educating disabled children were studied, and a resume is presented below:

Bangladesh developed a National Education Policy in 2000. The Education For All (EFA) plan aims at a 100% literacy rate by 2015, however disabled children are not included in this programme as their education is considered a welfare/charity issue. The 2001 Disability Welfare Act, for example, states that specialised educational institutions are required to cater for the special needs of different types of disabled children. It is stated in Bangladesh's PEDP-II (Primary Education Development programme-II) that mildly disabled children should be enrolled in primary schools, but this does not happen in practise. There is, in effect, no specific comprehensive policy and action plan regarding the education of disabled children.

Nepal's Education For All (EFA) plan aims to enrol all disabled children into the education system by 2015. However, there is no comprehensive education policy or action plan to include disabled children into mainstream schools. Nepal has a Special Needs Education Section (SNES) under it's Basic Primary Education Project-II. The SNES, in collaboration with DANIDA, initiated a pilot project on inclusive education including a 10 month teacher-training course.

Vietnam has a Disability Regulations and National EFA Action Plan, under which 70% of disabled children are to be in education by 2015, however there is no comprehensive action plan to ensure this will happen. Under the Ministry of Education and Training a Steering Committee on Inclusive Education (IE) has been formed and the Committee is in the process of developing an IE policy and strategy.

Following a long process the Republic of South Africa prepared a comprehensive plan - 'Education White Paper 6, Special Needs Education, Building an Inclusive Education and Training System'. This White Paper outlines what an Inclusive Education and Training educational system is, and provides the framework for establishing the system, including details of funding strategy, and the key steps required to take it forward. In addition South Africa has undertaken a pilot project on IE.

Key issues

The following issues became clear during the research and have an important bearing on the recommendations made, and conclusions reached at the end of the research period:

In all four countries the current educational systems established for disabled children are based on unreliable data about disability prevalence, problems faced by disabled children/learners and the educational needs of disabled children. By contrast, South Africa's recent (2001) Education White Paper 6 – 'Special Needs Education – Building an Inclusive Education and Training System' was drawn up following analysis of the current special needs and support services in education and training in South Africa. This will feed into the setting up of the proposed inclusive education system, but since this has not been established yet, it is not clear whether/how the data generated will shape the new inclusive system.

Stakeholders were asked to identify who they felt were the main 'duty bearers' responsible for ensuring the educational rights of disabled children. Government was identified as the primary duty bearer, followed by the family. This is significant in terms of drawing up and, probably more importantly, implementing, relevant legislation. In addition to this, as long as key stakeholders are not aware of the legislation, they will not hold governments to account for lack of implementation.

The concepts of all three systems differ between respondents and within the four countries. Whilst 'resource classes' in primary schools in Nepal are considered to be providing 'special education', the same system in Bangladesh is considered to be an integrated system.

Conclusion

The research in this area shows that educational services provided for disabled children are woefully inadequate in terms of not being able to cater for the numbers of disabled children there are. It is assumed that disabled children will not achieve intellectually or contribute to society in the same way as their non-disabled peers and that therefore vocational-based, segregated education is adequate for them. There is significant lack of motivation at government level to allocate human and financial resources to ensure implementation of current educational policies relevant to disabled children. An associated lack of public debate also exists about the appropriate nature or effectiveness of special education, given the current discussions and understandings of the social model of, and human rights approach to, disability. The social model of disability states that society 'disables' people, not their physical/intellectual impairments. The current educational provision for disabled children in the four countries researched shows this to be true. Disabled children are currently 'disabled' by systems that insist on defining them according to their impairment and not their intellectual capacity. Disabled children are seen as a problem for educational systems, and it should be the other way round.

INDEX